THE

MISSION-MINDED

CHILD

Ann Dunagan is the most effective and gifted children's teacher and motivator that I have come across in my lifetime. . . . Let her teach you—listen to her—she knows how and is now sharing it with others.

—DORIS GENE STEWART, forty years of experience as a missionary to Brazil and founder of an orphanage

I have known Jon and Ann Dunagan since 1987, and have had the privilege of being their friend, pastor, and fellow worker in the kingdom. . . . Jon and Ann are people of integrity, and I have confidence that God will continue to use them greatly in this generation.

—PASTOR NELS CHURCH, director of REAP International and missionary to the Philippines

We sincerely appreciate Ann's willingness to help raise the voice of the persecuted church.

—MYRTLE DODD, The Voice of the Martyrs

Ann Dunagan's writing is for those who want a heavy emphasis on world missions. . . . This book was not whipped up by a novice. The author is an evangelist's wife and homeschooling mother of seven who has ministered in more than twenty countries. She knows her stuff!

—VIRGINIA KNOWLES, Hope Chest Newsletter

We pray that *The Mission-Minded Child* will be a continued encouragement to your readers to God's glory.

—HELEN DAVIDSON, assistant to the director, The JESUS Film Project

Ann, may the Lord bless you in your publishing of this needed book. . . . We are truly hoping that the Lord will open our children's eyes and hearts to the tremendous harvest field that they may be called to work in someday. I know that living in a Third-World country broadens our perspectives and helps us to see the bigger picture of God's redemptive plan, so that's what we're praying for our children. May the Lord bless *The Mission-Minded Child* and your efforts for Him.

—VALERIE SHEPARD, pastor's wife and homeschooling mother, and daughter of Jim and Elisabeth Elliot

THE

MISSION-MINDED

CHILD

Raising a New Generation to
Fulfill God's Purpose

Ann Dunagan

Authentic

COLORADO SPRINGS · LONDON · HYDERABAD

Authentic Publishing
We welcome your questions and comments.

USA   1820 Jet Stream Drive, Colorado Springs, CO 80921 www.authenticbooks.com
UK   9 Holdom Avenue, Bletchley, Milton Keynes, Bucks, MK1 1QR
       www.authenticmedia.co.uk
India Logos Bhavan, Medchal Road, Jeedimetla Village, Secunderabad 500 055, A.P.

The Mission-Minded Child
ISBN-13: 978-1-932805-88-8
ISBN-10: 1-932805-88-5

Library of Congress Cataloging-in-Publication Data
Dunagan, Ann.
    The mission-minded child : raising a new generation to fulfill God's purpose / Ann Dunagan.
        p. cm.
    Includes bibliographical references and index.
    ISBN-13: 978-1-932805-88-8 (pbk. : alk. paper)
    ISBN-10: 1-932805-88-5 (pbk. : alk. paper) 1. Missions--Study and teaching. 2. Christian education--Home training. I. Title.

    BV2061.3.D86 2007
    266--dc22

                                    2007020562

Cover design: Paul Lewis
Interior design: Angela Lewis
Editorial team: Andy Sloan, Dana Bromley, KJ Larson

Printed in the United States of America

To my children:

Patrick, Joshua, Christine,
Daniel, Mark, Caela Rose, and Philip

You are God's mighty men and women!
May you hit the bull's-eye target of His destiny
and completely fulfill the exact mission
He has prepared for your life!

I love you!

Mom

"At no [other] time
is there greater capacity for devotion
or more pure, uncalculating ambition
in the service of God."

"When I am a man,
I mean to be a missionary
and go to China."

Contents

Appendix

The Mission-Minded Child Features

✒ Missions Poems and Hymns

(These are all appropriate for memory work and oratorical practice.)

📖 Missions Selections

🙎 Mini Missionary Biographies

(those marked with an asterisk include a "Mission-Minded Monologue Skit")

👫 From My Children's Perspective

🌐 Teaching Opportunities

How to Use This Book

This book is simply a tool to help you, as a Christian parent (or teacher), impart to the next generation a passion for Jesus Christ and a heart for God's mission to our world. It's not just information; it's inspiration!

- **Get inspired!** Browse through the pages for motivating missions stories, songs, poems, and examples to renew your own passion for the lost and God's eternally minded purpose for teaching and training your child.

- **Get missions facts!** Use it to reaffirm your missions foundation, to remember the world's need and our call to reach the lost, and to research a biblical basis for *why* we should share God's love with the nations.

- **Look things up!** This book is a quick missions resource manual, with mini missionary biographies, famous world mission quotes, and a helpful guide to locate great kid-friendly resources with mission-minded vision.

- **Find practical ideas!** Are you looking for easy-to-use missions ideas? This book includes sections on giving to missions, encouraging missionaries, and promoting missions in your local church, plus creative ideas for making missions fun!

- **Teach with a heart for missions!** This book is filled with ideas to incorporate a heart for world missions into nearly every subject. For English, there are missions selections to read aloud, classical excerpts for memory and oratorical practice, plus ideas to spark your child's creative writing. For geography and social studies, there are world maps, missions songs, and funny international stories. For a biblical foundation, there are Scripture verses to learn, prayer projects, and many practical ideas to encourage your child in solid Christian discipleship.

Note: Nearly all of the following mission stories and excerpts can be used for reading aloud to a child, although a few examples (due to difficult or graphic language) may be more appropriate to save until your child has grown into his or her teenage years. As a parent or teacher, please use your own judgment regarding the maturity of your child; and, in any case, let these stories and excerpts challenge *you*, as a mission-minded adult!

When I Was a Child . . .

I was eight years old when I first felt God's "call" to world missions.

I'll never forget the moment. It was a typical summer morning at Christian Renewal Center, a small family camp nestled in the midst of tall evergreens and majestic waterfalls. A teacher had encouraged my class to go out into the woods to pray and to ask God to simply "speak" to us from His Word.

So, taking my tattered children's Bible, I marched down a familiar dirt trail, sat down on a log, and began to pray.

Lord, is there anything you want to tell me?

I was quiet . . . but I didn't "hear" anything, except a small stream rippling beside me. *Would God ever talk to a young child like me?*

I tried to listen.

Just then, a strong thought came to my mind: *Look in Jeremiah.*

Gazing up through the trees, I wondered, *Was that from You, God?*

I knew "Jeremiah" was a book from the Old Testament, but it was in a part of the Bible I usually didn't understand. I assumed it would probably just be full of a bunch of "so-and-so begat so-and-so" type of verses.

But the thought didn't go away. *Look in Jeremiah, chapter one.*

Tentatively, I opened my Bible, found Jeremiah, and began to read. The verses started off like I had imagined they would—with big words and confusing names—but by the time I reached the fourth verse something of God's Holy Spirit began to well up inside me. As I continued reading, it felt like God Himself was talking directly to me.

> Then the word of the LORD came to me, saying: "Before I formed you in the womb I knew you; before you were born I sanctified you; I ordained you a prophet to the nations."
>
> Then said I: "Ah, Lord GOD! Behold, I cannot speak, for I am a youth."
>
> But the LORD said to me: "Do not say, 'I am a youth,' for you shall go to all to whom I send you, and whatever I command you, you shall speak. Do not be afraid of their faces, for I am with you to deliver you," says the LORD.
>
> Jeremiah 1:4–8

Two years later . . .

I was tagging along beside my mom at a Christian women's meeting when a lady came over and asked if she could pray for me. This woman didn't know me at all, but as she laid her hands on my head and started praying, she began quoting those same verses—"my" verses—from Jeremiah!

I was only ten years old, but once again it felt as if God was "speaking" directly to me—drawing me closer to Him and to the nations.

Tears welled up, as I began to cry. Inside, I just *knew* God was real, and those verses from Jeremiah *were* for me.

Thirty years later . . .

Not too long ago I was earnestly praying about this book, searching my motives, and trying to discern God's will. Unless I felt this project was something really "birthed" from the Lord for my life, I didn't want any part of it. In all honesty, I wasn't willing to sacrifice the time and energy I knew it would take if it could be better invested in my own children, in our home church, and in our missionary work.

But I kept feeling a stirring—and urgency—to challenge other parents and teachers that "we must instill a vision for missions in the next generation!"

I sought counsel and prayer and was shocked when my husband actually began encouraging me to write. (Years before, my writing had become consuming, and neither of us wanted *that* again!) Our pastor also prayed with us and felt a strong affirmation about my pursuing this project.

In my prayer journal, I poured out my heart to the Lord: "Father, if this idea for 'The Mission-Minded Child' is not of You, I'm willing to just let this 'baby' die. Please show me, Lord. Not my way, but Your way; not my plans, but Your plans."

Soon afterward I attended a church baby shower. During the refreshment time, I felt drawn to ask a certain elderly woman to pray for me. I didn't know much about her; I just knew she was a woman who prayed. As we talked by the punch bowl, she asked me to share more about my idea.

"It would be a book to impart a passion for world missions in parents and teachers," I explained, "to help raise a new generation of children and young people to fulfill God's Great Commission."

This precious lady then caught me by surprise. "Didn't you know?" she began. "World missions has been my life." She started to share a few of her stories. For nearly fifty years this amazing woman had served God as a missionary in Brazil. She had founded an orphanage, cared for 777 children, and placed them all in families. (And I had thought raising *seven* children was an accomplishment; I was in total awe of this woman's life!)

Right at that moment, our hostess (this woman's grown daughter, who I had just learned was one of the children from this orphanage) came over and asked if she could pray for me. Although she barely knew me, she believed God had shown her something in prayer several months earlier; but she had never felt a peace about sharing it with me—until now.

"As I've been praying for you, I feel like there's been a dream in your heart," the missionary's daughter began. "There's something you deeply wanted and worked on very hard, even through the middle of the night. For years you willingly laid it down—out of submission to your husband and out of submission to God; but now, I believe God is beginning to give it back to you." Then she began quoting the exact verses from Jeremiah that meant so much to me as a little girl!

Before I could stop myself, I unexpectedly burst into tears. The Lord's presence was so strong, I literally sobbed.

Surrounding me and supporting me—like midwives—were three godly women from around the world: the elderly missionary and her daughter (once an abandoned Brazilian orphan), plus a wonderful intercessor from Samoa (who had just arrived in our area that day and was the grandmother of the woman to whom we were giving the baby shower). Together we prayed for this book and interceded for God to raise up a new generation for missions.

Hours later, my husband said he had never seen me so overtaken by emotion—other than when I had given birth—and, spiritually speaking, that is almost what it felt like. I had been willing to totally surrender this idea; but, ironically, at an actual baby shower God confirmed in my heart that this "baby" was really "birthed" of Him.

The whole experience felt like a dream; and once again, I *knew* God was real. Those Jeremiah verses were not just for me, after all! God is calling a new generation of children and young people to the nations.

Acknowledgments

There are no words to express my thankfulness to God—my Heavenly Father, my Lord Jesus, and my precious Holy Spirit—for saving me!

I also thank the Lord for blessing me with my wonderful husband and family. Jon: I appreciate your integrity, leadership, and total heart to follow Jesus; and kids: your lives and examples have given me increased confidence to encourage others.

I want to honor my parents, Patrick and Judy Molitor, for raising me to fulfill God's purposes and to never give up on God's dreams; and Tom and Roberta Dunagan, for helping Jon and me to grasp more of God's love for the world through your sacrificial giving.

David and Renée Sanford (with Elizabeth Jones, Elizabeth Honeycutt, and Rebekah Clark) of Sanford Communications, Inc., I'm grateful for your "making it happen" expertise, and Volney James (with Andrew Sloan, Angela Lewis, and everyone at Authentic Media), I'm glad you "caught this vision" to help impact a new generation for missions.

I appreciate the prayers and support of our Harvest Ministry partners and NETS Ministers and the intercession of our Osanidde children. Thanks to Doris Stewart and Deloys from Brazil and my precious prayer-sisters: Nanci, Vicki, Lisa, Sue, and Carol. Thank you Christian Renewal Center and the Hansen family for providing a place where many, like me, have heard God's call; Jennifer for telling me to "Capture this side of the pancake!"; and Pastor Fritz and Wendi Stranz and my CCHR family for your loving support and mission-minded vision.

Last, I thank you for reading this book . . . and letting me share my heart.

What Is a Mission-Minded Child?

The famous missionary explorer David Livingstone once said, "This generation can only reach this generation." But will we raise our children to reach effectively *their* generation for Jesus Christ?

We should answer "Yes!", and *The Mission-Minded Child* is a motivational resource to help. We need to focus on God's calling for our lives and work *with* Him to help raise a new generation of young people totally committed to His plans. Every follower of Jesus (including every Christian child) should have a "life mission" aimed at finding God's purpose and fulfilling His potential.

Parents (and Christian teachers), do you realize how important you are? You have been placed in a strategic position to impact the next generation. Parenting children is more than a "duty," and educating children is more than a "job." If your vital role is perceived from God's perspective and fulfilled with a focus toward the Lord and those who aren't Christians yet, multitudes of mission-minded children could be motivated to live a God-centered life. Perhaps this book will even inspire you to reach your potential as well. Your child (and you!) could become today's Christian leader and tomorrow's world-changer.

The Mission-Minded Child is a Christian parent's (and teacher's) guide to world missions. It's filled with practical ideas and information. Included are mini missionary biographies, motivational missions stories, classic poems, international songs and hymns, and hundreds of easy-to-use ideas. Hopefully, it will become a resource you'll want to refer to again and again.

Yet *The Mission-Minded Child* is even more! It's filled with passion, zeal, and inspiration. Within these pages, you'll be encouraged to recognize God's potential in your child. You'll be challenged to release your child to God for His purposes, then motivated to effectively raise your child for God to fulfill His specific mission (whatever that may be).

Often an adult may ask a child, "What do you want to be when you grow up?" But as mission-minded parents and teachers, our typical question could have the potential of directing a child toward total obedience to God and complete surrender to His purposes. We *should* say, "Oh, I wonder what exciting plans God has prepared for your life? When you grow up, will you do whatever *God* wants you to do?"

A Mission-Minded Child

A mission-minded child . . . dreams of fulfilling God's destiny.

A mission-minded child . . . may want to become a missionary—or a teacher or a doctor or a newspaper reporter or a state governor or a pastor or a businessperson or an airplane pilot or an author or a florist or a mother—as long as it's what *God* wants!

A mission-minded child . . . prays for that next-door neighbor.

A mission-minded child . . . is not a picky eater!

A mission-minded child . . . takes home a photo magnet from the visiting missionary family and puts it on the kitchen refrigerator.

A mission-minded child . . . is healthy, active, and adventurous!

A mission-minded child . . . spends a summer night sleeping outside on the trampoline, gazes up at a sky filled with twinkling stars, and realizes God's plan is infinitely bigger than his or her own backyard.

A mission-minded child . . . imagines rollerblading on the Great Wall of China!

A mission-minded child . . . recognizes the names of David Livingstone, Amy Carmichael, Hudson Taylor, and Loren Cunningham.

A mission-minded child . . . knows how to use chopsticks.

A mission-minded child . . . has a reputation for thoroughly enjoying the Bible sword drills and memory verse contests at church.

A mission-minded child . . . puts extra money in the monthly missions offering and feels extra good inside.

A mission-minded child . . . thinks it could be fun to sleep in a mud hut in Africa!

A mission-minded child . . . reads all the way through the Bible by the age of ten (or eleven or twelve)—and is excited to start again!

A mission-minded child . . . stares at the photos in the new geography textbook or magazine and imagines climbing to the top of that Egyptian pyramid, snorkeling in those tropical-blue waters, and giving a new outfit to that poor boy with the ripped-up shirt.

A mission-minded child . . . befriends the new kid at school.

A mission-minded child . . . thinks beyond the "box" of what's merely expected and hopes to do something big, or something little, for God.

A mission-minded child . . . wants to obey (even when no one is looking).

A mission-minded child . . . loves Jesus!

🌐 TEACHING OPPORTUNITY

Creative Writing Idea—Mission-Minded Statements

Read aloud the "A mission-minded child . . ." statements above and talk with your child about what it means to have a mission-minded heart. Encourage your child to write his or her own "A mission-minded child . . ." statements that share a heart for God and for His love for people all throughout the world.

Part I

Our Child and God's Plans

CHAPTER 1

Releasing Your Child to God

As Hannah embraced her little Samuel one last time, what thoughts must have filled her mind? As she placed his timid fingers into the hands of the old priest, Eli, . . . and let go, . . . what questions did she surrender to the Lord?

As Hannah looked back toward her home, what did her mother's heart feel? How could she walk away from the answer to all her prayers? How could she release this dream she had so desperately longed for—this dream that was now a real little boy looking up at her with questioning eyes and a quivering lip, trying to obey her loving instructions, and trying to hold back his tears?

If only Hannah could have known at that moment how the story looks from *our* perspective. We know her Samuel would soon hear the audible voice of God, he would impact the entire nation of Israel, and this very act of her obedient surrender would be recorded and recalled for generations.

But Hannah didn't know the future. She only knew it was time to say goodbye and go home—childless once again. She must have turned her face quickly so Samuel wouldn't see her mixed emotions.

As Hannah walked away, she released her little one into the mighty hand of God and chose to worship. As she did, God's plan began to unfold. For this child was not just Hannah's dream; he was God's dream. At the time, the nation of Israel desperately needed a new spiritual leader, and God had found a mother desperate enough for Him to willingly yield to His plans.

As parents or Christian teachers, we don't always realize the importance of our vital role in the kingdom of God. Will we equip our children to fulfill God's purposes and to reach for God's potential? Will we train our children to reach their world for Jesus?

Through this book I desire to light a spark for world missions that will grow into a fire for the unsaved like you've never had before. I want God's love for unreached people to burn so strongly inside you that it will start spreading to others, specifically to your own children and to the young people you come in contact with.

Over the years I've seen many of our world's appalling needs. I've had opportunities to travel and minister in dozens of countries. However, in this particular season of my life I'm primarily called to be at home. I love being a mother, raising a family, and teaching children. But sometimes, I admit, I get frustrated.

Many days I wonder if I am "doing" anything of significance and I often struggle with a horrible "striving" mentality in my flesh. When I hear of "big needs"—like the "big need" for world missions—I feel a striving to want to do something "important" (for God, of course!).

I want to be busy!

I want to go!

But sometimes it feels like I'm meeting only insignificant "little needs"—like sweeping the kitchen floor over and over, reading that naptime story (again!), and simply watching my children grow.

Yet, deep inside, I *do* know the truth. Raising and training children *is* important! "Striving," or mere "busyness," is not the same as "fruitfulness," and all God *really* requires is for me to stay close to Him and obey Him, day by day.

Today the Lord is simply showing me to be faithful—that is, to love God and to support my husband here at home; to be fruitful—to be a mother and to teach and train our children in the ways of the Lord; and to keep my eyes on the future—to eagerly anticipate the Lord's return and keep living in His joy.

As parents and teachers, we must "train up a child in the way he should go" (Proverbs 22:6), and in the Great Commission; Jesus said the way we should go is "into all the world and preach the gospel" (Mark 16:15).

David Livingstone said, "God had only one Son, and He made Him a missionary." Jesus came as our missionary to earth. He relinquished everything in heaven to provide the way for us (and all people) to come into relationship with Him. He knew the cost before Him, and the price He paid was beyond anything we could imagine.

In Hebrews 12:2, the Bible says we are to look to Jesus, "the author and finisher of our faith, who for the joy that was set before Him endured the cross, despising the shame." Jesus' incredible love compelled Him to the cross. His burning desire was to fully obey the will of the Father, providing a way for humanity to be reconciled back to God. Jesus was willing to sacrifice whatever it took: His position in heaven, His unsurpassed riches and glory, His reputation, and even His very life. Jesus was whipped, beaten, tortured, and despised—all for the *joy* that was set before Him.

Isaiah 9:2–3 describes the joy of harvest as a light shining through darkness. There is rejoicing when a lost coin is found! There is joy when a shepherd finds a lost sheep or when a prodigal finally comes home! Luke 15:7 tells us that "there will be more joy in heaven over one sinner who repents than over ninety-nine just persons who need no repentance."

This is the joy that led Jesus to the cross.

How many of us are so captivated by God's love that we would be willing to lay down everything to follow Him?

We should take a moment to consider our lives and our priorities from God's eternal perspective:

• As we teach and train our children, what are we hoping they will achieve?

- As we steward God's resources, what are we saving toward?

- As we influence the next generation, what dreams are we instilling?

- As we talk to God, what is the primary focus of our prayers?

As Christians, we must realize that God's love, His passionate love, resides in us. Are we willing to allow this love to flow through us (and through our children) to the world? Second Corinthians 5:14–15 says, "For the love of Christ compels us . . . that those who live should live no longer for themselves, but for Him who died for them and rose again."

Like Hannah, we must realize that our child is actually God's child—entrusted to us for only a short time. We need to release our child to God and then follow His guidance to raise His child for His divine purposes!

My prayer is for the simple words in this book to penetrate deep into your soul and spirit. I know you don't need more information; but we all need more inspiration. I pray that God's love for the world will someday explode in your heart like a blast of dynamite. I hope you will begin to be moved by the things that move God's heart and that you will allow God's precious Holy Spirit to impart this heart into your child.

We've all heard the famous saying, "The hand that rocks the cradle rules the world." I say, "May the child in our cradle (or our classroom) *reach* the world . . . for the One who rules it all!"

"A KID'S HEART FOR MISSIONS"

By Joshua Dunagan, at age seven

I wrote this letter and drew this picture about ten years ago when I was about seven years old. My spelling and handwriting is embarrassing, but it does show how God can give a vision for missions—even to a kid.

God, I love You. Thank You for dying on the cross for my sins and that You rose from the dead, Lord. When I grow up, I will do anything You want me to do, Lord. Even if You want me to go and preach into dangerous places, Lord.

Joshua

CHAPTER 2

Raising Your Child for God

*"Train up a child in the way he should go
[and in keeping with his individual gift or bent],
and when he is old he will not depart from it."*
—*Proverbs 22:6 (AMPLIFIED)*

Missions is not an isolated "subject" to study, but an attitude and an exciting (although challenging) way of looking at our entire world! Just as Christianity influences every aspect of our lives, so also should God's heart for the lost completely change our outlook and our priorities.

Hudson Taylor was very young when his parents imparted to him a passionate heart for Jesus and a lifelong commitment to missions. Speaking of childhood, Taylor's parents said, "At no [other] time is there greater capacity for devotion or more pure, uncalculating ambition in the service of God." At only five years of age, Hudson Taylor often said, "When I am a man, I mean to be a missionary and go to China." Was it merely a coincidence that this little boy grew to become one of China's greatest missionaries? No, this childhood dream was God's purpose, diligently nurtured by godly parents.

It's a great responsibility to "train up a child in the way he should go." We begin by training our little one to walk and talk; as our child grows older, we help with reading and writing; and as the years go by, more and more aspirations are added to our agenda—as diverse as encouraging academics and musical skills to cheering at athletic events and monitoring young friends. All along the way, we work hard to instill in our child a deep love for the Lord. We want our child to be a young person with godly character, to have a heart of purity, to desire God's specific plan, and to fully obey Him in whatever way He leads.

I want to challenge you in this calling. The purpose for this book is to provide a practical and encouraging resource. I hope to inspire you to a deeper personal level of commitment to God's Great Commission and to equip you to impart effectively His heart to your child.

Around the world, the need for the gospel is beyond what most of us can even comprehend. Most of us are usually so bogged down with busyness and unending responsibilities that it's an accomplishment just to keep afloat here at home. The idea of traveling across the seas to "rescue souls" is something we try not to think about, but maybe we need to think about the real boys and girls and men and women who have yet to hear about Jesus Christ.

Q. Are you a Christian parent?

- **Public (or Private Non-Christian) School Parents**—Nearly every parent wants to raise his or her child to succeed in life and to find true purpose. For many Christian families, a public (or private non-Christian) school education is the path chosen to reach this goal. Yet a Christian child's true purpose or "mission" will not be found in any book or in any school. True success in God's eyes will come only from a child's personal devotion to God and a practical obedience to His will.

  Beginning in the early educational years, many God-loving children embark on their first "missionary adventure" by going to school. Sometimes, however, impressionable children are influenced for evil more than their peers are influenced for good. We need to guard our child in order to withstand the predominantly non-Christian worldviews within many school systems. As mission-minded parents, we need to provide a strong prayer covering and make sure that our child has a steadfast commitment to Jesus Christ and a sincere concern for those who don't know Christ yet.

By encouraging our child's faith and strengthening our child's own relationship with the Lord, he or she will more easily find God's mission—and fulfill it!

- **Christian School Parents**—If your child attends a Christian school you are likely investing a great deal of money each month to provide your child with a biblically based education. As a Christian school parent, you obviously care deeply about your child receiving godly instruction; yet you can't delegate the ultimate responsibility for your child's spiritual training to anyone else. God places the primary child-raising responsibility on the parents, so it is necessary to take time to check up on your educational investment and ensure that the spiritual training your child is receiving at school and at church is supplemented with a strong biblical foundation from your own home.

Q. Are you a home educator?

All throughout the world today, millions of children are being taught at home. A majority of these homeschooling families are Christians, and many of these parents strongly desire to teach with a biblical worldview. This makes for an excellent foundation for mission-minded training.

One of the greatest challenges many missionary families encounter is the education of their children, but homeschoolers are already prepared! If the Lord would call a homeschool family to foreign missionary service, their children's education could continue nearly the same as before (simply exchanging their kitchen table at home for one overseas). And if the Lord would call a homeschooled child to missionary work, a parent could specifically tailor that child's education to help him or her prepare. Even the idea of world travel sets a homeschooling parent's mind racing with exciting opportunities for international field trips and hands-on geography lessons!

In addition, homeschool families are accustomed to making sacrifices in many areas of life. They're already considered "a little radical" for going against the flow of traditional education; they often think "outside the box" of what's possible; and they're usually spending hours together as a family—reading, exploring new ideas, and continually seeking God's will. Homeschooling and a heart for world missions can make a great combination!

Each Christian family must earnestly seek God's will for the education of their children and obey God's direction—whatever that may be. Strong mission-minded children can be found in Christian schools, in public schools, and in home-based schools.

Q. Are you a teacher in a church or Christian school?

If so, God needs you!

God needs mission-minded educators in every Christian school, in every church program, and in every Sunday school! A heart for world missions should be a vital part of every Christ-centered classroom and included in every child's spiritual training.

As a Christian teacher, your potential in the kingdom of God is great! Year after year, classroom after classroom, you are in a position of leadership that can influence the hearts of many children. Through you, or through one young person you train, God could someday transform a community, city, or nation.

Q. Are you even the "missions type"?

"World missions" is something I am passionate about. A portion of this book was actually written in Tanzania and Uganda while I was on a missionary outreach in Africa. In the midst of children's ministry and women's seminars, visiting village churches, and helping with city-wide evangelistic meetings, I was thinking about this book—and you, the reader—and praying for ways to effectively impart God's compassion for the world.

In light of that, some of you may have compartmentalized me into some stereotypical missionary box in your mind and think that you and I have nothing in common. You may not consider yourself the "missions type" at all.

But please let me redefine "missions." You (and your child) are specially designed by God, who has an individualized "mission" for your life. There is absolutely no one else just like you; and no one else can fulfill the unique God-given mission He has planned just for you. As followers of Jesus Christ we are all called—every one of us—to the mission of expanding God's kingdom.

How "missions" looks in your life—or how it will look in the life of each child—may be very different than how it looks in my life. Or perhaps it may look similar.

You may even discover that you and I have more in common than you realize. In day-to-day life, I actually consider myself a very "normal" Christian:

- I'm a follower of Jesus, and I love my Lord.

- I'm a parent, and I love my children.

- I'm a teacher, and I love to teach. (Well, most of the time!)

Perhaps like you, my daily "missions adventures" include many not-so-glamorous expeditions—such as battling bedroom disasters, tackling insurmountable laundry piles, celebrating a successful potty-training moment, or attacking a stack of schoolwork that needs to be graded. I've had exciting and encouraging teaching experiences, but I continue to struggle with daily disciplines and feelings of inadequacy—especially when homeschooling my teenagers!

Over the past twenty years, God has graciously provided opportunities for my husband and me (along with our children) to travel and minister in many international outreaches all across the globe. By seeing the world's needs for ourselves, our perspective has simply changed—and these experiences have drastically impacted our philosophy of raising and teaching children.

Our Lord's Great Commission is much more than an isolated memory verse. Loving Jesus and reaching those who don't have a relationship with Him is the central core of all we do.

As you read this book, may God begin to unveil His incredible love for the unreached and help you impart a new zeal for missions into the heart of your child. Whatever purpose God has planned—whether your child is called to be a medical doctor, a political leader, a successful businessperson, a teacher, a missionary, or a parent—may each child God entrusts to you be raised as His mission-minded child.

 TEACHING OPPORTUNITY

Missions Memory, Oratorical Practice, and Object Lesson (Life Line)

Encourage your child to read the classic missions poem and hymn, "A Passion for Souls." Look up words your child might not be familiar with (such as *passion*, *adored*, and *pardon*), and explain the concept of a lifeguard who throws a "life line" to a person who is drowning. (For an object lesson, you could give your child a LifeSavers® candy or hold up a life preserver, life jacket, or blow-up flotation device as you teach this point.) Have your child memorize this poem and practice reciting it with clear enunciation as he or she speaks every word with feeling and conviction.

A PASSION FOR SOULS

A missions poem and hymn, by Herbert G. Tovey, 1888

Give me a passion for souls, dear Lord,
A passion to save the lost;
O that Thy love were by all adored,
And welcomed at any cost.

Jesus, I long, I long to be winning
Men who are lost, and constantly sinning;
O may this hour become of beginning
The story of pardon to tell. . . .

How shall this passion for souls be mine?
Lord, make Thou the answer clear;
Help me to throw out the old life line
To those who are struggling near.

Part II

Our Foundation for the Nations

CHAPTER 3

Our Call

For many Christians, "missions" is, at best, a necessary responsibility. For hundreds of years the church has always "supported the missionaries," and so tradition continues—yet often without God's heart and passion or even a compelling purpose to win boys and girls, men and women to faith in Jesus Christ.

No wonder, then, when many of us think of a missionary, strange images come to mind!

You may picture some young adventurer—clad in khaki safari clothes—trudging through the jungles with a machete. Perhaps you imagine him (or her) meeting a group of dark-skinned natives, dancing around mud huts and a raging fire, all moving to the beat of a pounding tribal drum. Or maybe your only view of a missionary is of some strange older couple, in outdated clothing, presenting never-ending blurry slides or a shaky home video for some "special" Sunday evening service. Completing this picture are uninspiring stories of terrible food and awful living conditions, ending with that dreaded drawn-out plea for money.

Perhaps, for the sake of our children, it's time to change our pictures of missions today.

Q. Is there still a need for world missions?

The word *mission* brings to mind synonyms such as *goal, vision,* and *purpose.* As Christians, what is God's purpose for our lives? What are His goals and vision?

- **Our primary calling** . . . is to know and love the Lord. But if that were all, God could have taken us to heaven the moment we received Jesus Christ.

- **Our primary mission** . . . is to glorify God in and through our lives and to help make God known throughout the earth.

With our primary mission clearly in view, it's obvious we need to help proclaim the gospel of Jesus Christ and obey God's words to "Go into all the world." We need to ask ourselves if we really believe the Bible is the true and inspired Word of God. Do we honestly believe people must be saved, or "born again," as Jesus said in John 3:3, and can we comprehend the eternal reality of heaven and hell? If we do, these beliefs should radically impact our lives.

Think for a moment about how different your life would be if you were born in a land isolated from God and filled with extreme poverty, sickness, and disease. What would it be like if you were born in an area where praying to an idol or giving homage to an ancestor was your only hope? What if constant fear of evil spirits consumed your life? Wouldn't you want someone to share God's life-giving message of salvation with *you*?

We have received God's light, but it is not just for us. We're called to shine God's light in the darkness.

For those of us who live in developed countries, we need to realize how much God has blessed us.

- **We are blessed!** Every day we enjoy clean, hot running water—without a thought.

- **We are blessed!** Our typical meals often include ingredients from all around the world: fruit from California and the Polynesian islands, olive oil from Italy and the Middle East, and perhaps coffee from Columbia (just try looking at your food labels for a few days). We eat better than the ancient kings!

- **We are blessed!** Most of us, with only a few quick calls to a credit card company and a local travel agency, could likely travel next month to any destination in the world if we really wanted to (not that I'm advocating debt, but if reaching people is our priority, our budgets can be made to accommodate).

God has given us the greatest "Good News" of all time and a job description to "Get this news out!" He has given us an abundance of resources to accomplish the task and a challenge that "To whom much is given, from him much will be required" (Luke 12:48).

TEACHING OPPORTUNITY

Creative Writing Idea—List God's Blessings

Have your child make a list of some of the blessings God has given. Encourage your child to try to list one item for each letter of the alphabet. Another idea is to look through magazines and cut out pictures of typical blessings that we sometimes take for granted.

Q. Why go overseas when we have so many needs in our own country?

Missionary evangelist Oswald J. Smith answered this question with another: "Why should anyone hear the gospel twice before everyone has heard it once?"

We do have needs, but ours pale in comparison, according to the *World Christian Encyclopedia*:

- **The missions need:** In North America there are more than one million full-time Christian workers (one full-time Christian leader for every 230 people), while in many places there is only one missionary for every 500,000 people!

- **The missions need:** Out of all the finances given to the Christian church worldwide, 96.8 percent is spent on those who have already received Christ (Christians spending money on Christians), 2.9 percent is spent on those who have heard but rejected the gospel, and only 0.3 percent is spent on reaching those who have never once heard God's Good News.

- **The missions need:** Since the invention of the printing press in 1450, 85 percent of all Bibles ever printed have been printed in English—yet only 9 percent of the world speaks that language! An estimated 80 percent of the world's population has never owned a Bible, while in the United States, for example, there is an average of four Bibles in every household.

- **The missions need:** Many of us hear the gospel again and again, while approximately 1.6 billion people are still waiting for their first opportunity to hear.

- **The missions need:** Even among Christian missionaries, only 15 percent of all missionary finances are used for gospel work among "unreached" people. *Revolution in World Missions* states that nearly 80 percent of all missionaries are involved primarily in social work, not in proclaiming the gospel, winning souls, or establishing churches. For heaven's sake— literally—what did Jesus call us to do?

Q. Aren't all cultures equally valid? Why should we try to change other people's cultures?

The core issue of this question stems from a false application of "multiculturalism"—one that is politically correct, educationally encouraged, and sounds nice. But leaving people trapped in sin and isolated from God's hope of salvation isn't the "considerate" option.

As Christians, we bring the cross-cultural, life-changing message of Jesus Christ and His forgiveness for sin. Our purpose is not to propagate our own cultural standards, but to present the gospel in a redeeming yet culturally sensitive way to all people we meet. Eliminating the beautiful uniqueness of international culture is not the purpose of missions; at times, however, sinful elements of a particular culture may need to change.

I will never forget an interview I had with an outstanding Christian teenager who attended a public high school. This young man led a lunchtime "Bible Club" and worship time that grew to reach 250 of his fellow classmates. He was writing a school research paper on Christian missionary work and, specifically, he was trying to support his thesis that "modern missionaries do not attempt to 'change' foreign cultures."

I understood this young man's heart. He was trying to explain how today's Christian missionaries are different—more culturally appreciative and sensitive—than some of the old-time colonial missionaries (who attempted to expand all aspects of Western civilization throughout the world). But I still disagreed with his conclusion.

I asked this young man a pointed question. "But don't you try to 'change the culture' of the people you are trying to reach? Just look at the typical 'culture' of the teens in your high school before they come to Jesus Christ! Look at the way they dress! Listen to their music, their foul language, and the way they address their teachers! What about the videos they watch and the movies they sneak into? What about typical teenagers involved in sexual impurity or the girls who've had abortions? Aren't all of these a part of teen 'culture'?"

I went on to explain to him, "Culture is *life*! When you share Jesus Christ in your high school, of course you don't want your friends to stop being teenagers—that's who they are! But you *do* want Jesus Christ to totally transform the way they live and the way they make their decisions!"

Around the world, societies that have developed isolated from God's laws and the gospel are filled with sinful cultural elements:

- tribal hatred, ancestral worship, and idolatry

- immoral sex, adultery, and prostitution

- drug addiction, drunkenness, and witchcraft

- abuse and neglect of women and children

As Christians, our job is to bring the light of Jesus to every precious culture. Through His Word and His Holy Spirit, God will show people the changes they need to make to redeem their cultures back to Him.

Q. Why go to those remote foreign tribes? Wouldn't they probably be "better off" just left as they are?

My answer to that question is a loud "No! No! No!" The unreached are never better off without Jesus Christ! Often we are blinded to this fact by a movie-world version of a "tropical native paradise." Some influential films and books portray remote tribes living in "peaceful bliss and harmony" until some "big, bad missionary" comes on the scene. But this paradise is only an illusion!

By God's grace I have personally ministered throughout Latin America and the Caribbean, North America, Eastern and Western Europe, Asia, Africa, and Australia—from remote villages to crowded inner cities. Throughout these missionary travels I have never seen this "tropical native paradise"! At times, the land and beaches *are* beautiful and people may be warm and friendly; yet lives without God are always filled with misery.

- **In the Philippines** . . . I remember walking through a squatters' village and seeing streams of human waste flowing openly down a path. I was horrified to watch a group of Filipino children toss a bucket of garbage into an already dirty river, jump in the middle of it, and start throwing the garbage on each other. These poor children were just playing, oblivious to the filth and potential for disease. Although yes, it was tropical, it was so far from God's garden of Eden!

- **In Costa Rica** . . . I saw people crawl on bloody bare knees in penance for their sins. In Guatemala, I sadly watched as crowds of poor, devoted people surrendered large sums of money just to carry a religious icon. These people were desperate for God's forgiveness, but as I looked into their faces I saw no joy and no assurance of salvation.

- **In Uganda** . . . My husband and I once ministered to a tribe of people who actually worshiped a large tree. These Africans were aware of their sins and even the need for the shedding of innocent blood; yet their religion gave them no hope. They blindly offered animal sacrifices to this tree and, as I was told, at times, even the human sacrifices of their young children.

- **In Tanzania** . . . In 1995 my husband and I were ministering in a remote city when one morning we heard horrifying news. Radical Muslims had bombed the city grounds where we were scheduled to sing, preach, and show the *JESUS* film. In the process, these terrorists destroyed a primary school—killing eight precious children and seriously wounding eighty others (most who eventually died)—all to protest the message of Christianity.

- **Across the globe** . . . Throughout history—in places such as Nazi Germany, Rwanda, Bosnia, Ethiopia, and Iraq—government systems have planned for the elimination of entire people groups. Twisted religious beliefs (such as the Hindu reverence of the cow and the rat) have caused self-inflicted food shortages and starvation. Many isolated people groups are bound by fear, controlled by witchcraft, or filled with tribal hatred.

All over the world, individuals without Christ are separated from God by sin and are destined to spend eternity even further separated from Him—unless they hear and respond to God's Good News! Our Lord Jesus Christ came to destroy this barrier of sin. He surrendered His life on the cross and sacrificed His perfect, sinless blood so that all people could have access to God's eternal life in heaven.

The entire message of the Bible can be summarized in words we all likely know by heart: "For God so loved the world that He gave His only begotten Son, that whoever believes in Him should not perish but have everlasting life" (John 3:16).

Q. Are the "lost" *really* lost?

In one of my favorite movies, *Anne of Avonlea*, I've often replayed the scene where two elderly friends, Marilla Cuthbert and Rachel Lynde, are knitting together on the front porch of Anne's house, Green Gables. As Mrs. Lynde refers to some "heathenness" murder trials from a Boston newspaper, she declares, "Can you imagine that new minister, going on about how he doesn't believe that all the heathen will be eternally lost? The idea! If they won't be, all the money we've been sending to the foreign missions will be completely wasted, that's what!"

It's a simple excerpt, but a big issue. As Christians, what we believe about the spiritual and eternal condition of those who don't have a relationship with God greatly affects our attitude toward world missions.

Today the word *heathen* has a negative connotation and is considered an outdated term; yet this word's meaning delves deep into our core theology of world missions. The term refers not only to people who are unsaved but specifically to "unreached people who have *never* heard the gospel." Is our true motivation for missions to share the Good News of Jesus Christ with those who have yet to hear it, or do we merely want to help poor people live a better life? What makes *God's* calling to reach the world any different than a government assistance program or a secular benevolence outreach? The bottom-line distinction is our belief about the lost and especially our convictions about these people who have never heard the gospel.

Are these lost people *really* lost, or does God have an "alternative way" for them to be saved? The question makes us very uneasy and very uncomfortable. We wonder, "How could a good God send people to hell just because they've never heard the gospel?"

It seems so unfair. But to answer this question we need to look beyond what *we think* and what *we feel* about fairness to what *we can know* from God's Word.

First of all, people are not separated from God because they have never heard the gospel; people are separated from God because of sin. This sin includes both the sins we ourselves commit and the "sin nature" that has been passed down to all humanity ever since Adam and Eve's fall in the garden of Eden. Isaiah 53:5 states, "He was wounded for our transgressions, He was bruised for our iniquities." When Jesus Christ died on the cross, He totally paid the penalty price for both our sins and our human sin nature.

The lost in foreign countries are not innocent. They have sinned and will be judged before our absolutely perfect holy God. We can trust God to judge righteously, and we can trust what He has shown us in His Word. The Bible tells us, "For all have sinned . . ." (Romans 3:23); and deep down, everyone knows it. Even without knowledge of God's laws and the gospel message, a person inwardly knows that he or she has done wrong things. Everyone has violated the inborn, God-placed convictions of his or her own conscience (although some have violated these convictions so many times that their hearts may have become calloused and they no longer feel remorse or guilt). This inborn realization of sin is one of the primary reasons why much of humanity is so religious. All around the world people are desperately trying to do something about their sin (even if they are only desperately trying to ignore God's tug on their hearts).

So are those without the Good News *really* lost, or can a person's "ignorance" of the gospel exempt him or her from the consequences of sin? Consider the second alternative: If total ignorance (of the message of

God's salvation through Jesus Christ) was an alternative way to heaven, why wouldn't it be best to keep everyone ignorant? With this reasoning, if everyone was ignorant, everyone could be spared! Why not take it a step further and destroy all Bibles and eliminate evangelism? Then the entire world could be "saved" through this "guaranteed-ignorance exemption."

But obviously, this is not God's way.

If before the gospel came everyone was "ignorant" (but on their way to heaven), and after the gospel came everyone would have "knowledge" of God's salvation (but could then be condemned to hell), then wouldn't the Good News message actually be Very Bad News to a previously unreached people group? But Jesus Christ knew—more than any of us could ever know—that salvation through His perfect sacrifice was (and is) humankind's only hope. The night before Jesus was crucified, he desperately cried to His Father in the garden of Gethsemane, "If it is possible, let this cup pass from Me; nevertheless, not as I will, but as You will" (Matthew 26:39).

If there was any other way for human beings to be saved, then why did God allow Jesus to go to the cross? It is because there was (and is) no other way.

Without God's salvation—on His terms and only through the cross of His only Son—the "lost" are desperately and completely lost. Only the blood of Jesus Christ can eliminate our record of sin and pay the price that the consequence of sin requires before God. Remember the words of the old hymn: *What can wash away my sin? Nothing but the blood of Jesus!*

This fact led Jesus to the cross. This fact motivated early missionaries to leave their homelands with no hope of return; this fact was a passionate force behind the sacrificial giving of previous generations; and this fact motivates millions of Christians today. It's a vital missions fact that we must instill—with conviction—in the hearts and minds of the next generation.

The fact is: without Jesus Christ, the lost *are* lost.

And although Jesus' death was sufficient to pay in full the penalty price for every person's sins, not everyone is saved, or redeemed. Each person is required to come to God individually through faith in Jesus Christ and claim God's gift of salvation for himself or herself.

🌐 TEACHING OPPORTUNITY

Mission-Minded Object Lesson (Coupons)

Have you ever received a package of grocery coupons or a free gift certificate? Just because you possess a coupon for something does not necessarily guarantee that you will ever receive the product. Hold up a grocery store coupon as you read this analogy about God's gift of salvation.

- ### *Free Doughnut Coupons:*

Suppose a nationwide grocery store chain decides to promote a certain new brand of doughnuts. The company produces millions upon millions of "free doughnut coupons" and pays the postal service to deliver coupons to every resident in the country. Each person would be eligible for a dozen doughnuts; to receive a free box of doughnuts, however, each person must go to the grocery store and "redeem" his or her coupon. Those who don't redeem their coupons won't get any doughnuts, and thus their unused coupon is worthless.

Unfortunately some people, for one reason or another, do not have a coupon. Perhaps the mailing never reached their home. Perhaps some international residents didn't understand English and were unable to read their coupon. Perhaps some people were too busy and their coupon got lost. Perhaps others couldn't care less about a free box of doughnuts and simply threw their coupon away.

The reasons really don't matter. The point is, unless a person receives a coupon, he will likely know nothing about the special offer; and unless a person takes her coupon to the store to get it "redeemed," she will not get any doughnuts.

The lost must hear.

This fact should compel us to our knees and draw us to the nations.

Is it fair? No.

Is it fair that Jesus had to die in our place? No.

Is it fair that we go to our churches week after week . . . and year after year . . . when multitudes have never even heard once that Jesus came?

Is it fair that we sit on padded pews and critique our pastor's polished sermons, while over 1.6 billion people have never heard even one simple gospel message?

No. It is not fair. But God is totally good and holy and just. He has never been "obligated" to save the lost, and He was not even "obligated" to save us! It is only because of God's great grace that He offers us His salvation, and it is only because of God's great love that He now passionately urges and compels us to proclaim this salvation—God's great news.

🌐 TEACHING OPPORTUNITY

Object Lesson and Mission-Minded Prayer Project (Clock)

Second Peter 3:9 tells us that God is "not willing that any should perish but that all should come to repentance." And He has given us the job of sharing His message of hope and Good News. To help explain this need to your child, emphasize Christ's love and His sacrifice on the cross for the sins of the world. To set a more serious tone, you and your child could watch a second hand on a clock for exactly one minute as you share how every sixty seconds (according to current statistics) nearly one hundred people die (which totals about 150,000 people every day), and the vast majority have not received God's salvation through Jesus Christ. Emphasize the importance of having God's heart for the lost, and then encourage your child to pray for people who don't know Jesus. Use the clock again to pray—fervently and compassionately—for exactly one minute for God to send missionaries to these people who need Jesus.

A HUNDRED THOUSAND SOULS***

Unknown

A hundred thousand souls a day
Are passing, passing fast away,
In Christless guilt and gloom;
Oh Church of Christ, what wilt thou say,
When in the awful Judgment Day,
They charge thee with their doom?

*** Author's Note: These vital mission concepts of death, dying, hell, and the unsaved (along with this classic mission poem) will likely be too traumatic for a younger child. Parents and teachers should seek the Lord's discretion and guidance to know when these biblical truths should be appropriately introduced.

> "Every man, woman, and child in heathen darkness
> is a challenge to the church."
>
> S. E. TAYLOR

 THE LITTLE STARFISH

A mission story to read aloud to children

One day an old man was walking along the beach at low tide. Across the sand he could see thousands upon thousands of starfish drying in the sun. He knew they would soon die, but he thought nothing of it.

As he continued to walk he noticed, far ahead, a child throwing something into the water. Coming closer, the man could see a young boy hurriedly tossing starfish—one by one—into the ocean waves.

"Why are you working so hard?" the man asked the boy. "Can't you see how many starfish are still on the sand? What difference could it make?"

The boy looked down at the starfish in his hand, and then looked up. "Well, Sir," he humbly responded, "it'll make a difference to this one."

And with that, he threw the little starfish into the water.

TEACHING OPPORTUNITY

Mission-Minded Discussion (Starfish Story)

Read the story of "The Little Starfish" with your child and discuss the importance of doing what we can to help others. We will never be able to meet *every* need in the world, but with God's help we can make a difference in the lives of some people, one by one.

Discussion Questions:

1. What does this story about the little starfish represent?

2. Do you know anyone like the little boy? Or like the old man?

3. Who should we be more like?

4. How can we be "starfish savers"?

5. Can you think of a specific person we can help?

CHAPTER 4

Our Biblical Basis

Matthew 28:19–20 and Mark 16:15 are often referred to as "The Great Commission." These final words of Jesus to "Go therefore and make disciples of all the nations . . ." and to "Go into all the world and preach the gospel . . ." are often memorized and sometimes overly familiar; but the biblical basis for world missions reaches far beyond these two verses! God's heart for the world—and our obligation as His followers to take the gospel to the ends of the earth —is a central theme throughout the entire Word of God.

World Missions from Genesis to Revelation!

We can see God's compassion for *all* people in Israel's invasion of Jericho which was led by Joshua. By faith, a prostitute in Jericho named Rahab believed in God and extended a scarlet cord through her window on the wall. By faith, she and all her loved ones gathered in her house were saved from destruction.

I don't think it was just a coincidence that the color of Rahab's rope was red. I see this "scarlet cord" as a powerful object lesson of God's grace and mercy that extends to all people—and as a recurring illustration of God's truth that is intertwined throughout the Bible, from Genesis to Revelation, and ultimately fulfilled in our Lord Jesus Christ.

We see our first glimpse of this "scarlet cord" when God clothes Adam and Eve with the skins of an innocent animal after sin enters the world. We see it during the Passover deliverance as God saved the Israelites by instructing them to put the blood of the lamb over their doorways and specified a way for the "strangers" (or Gentiles) living among them to celebrate the Passover (see Exodus 12:48). We see it in the book of Daniel as God reveals Himself to the mighty kings of Babylon and Persia, and we see it interwoven throughout the prophecies of Isaiah and Jeremiah. This "scarlet cord" is found in God's unrelenting call to Jonah and the people of the wicked city of Nineveh and throughout many of David's psalms.

Jesus' Heart for All Nations

It's true that a person's last words are important, but God's heart and focus did not suddenly change as Jesus Christ ascended into heaven. As He rose into the clouds, it wasn't as if Jesus dropped some last-minute change of plans on His followers: "Oh, by the way, there's just one major thing I forgot to tell you. . . ."

When Jesus came to earth, His birth was announced to Jews (the shepherds) and to Gentiles (the wise men) as an angel brought "good tidings of great joy which will be to all people" (Luke 2:10). As Jesus was dedicated in the temple, Simeon's prophetic word included, "My eyes have seen Your salvation which You have prepared before the face of all peoples, a light to bring revelation to the Gentiles" (Luke 2:30–32).

During Jesus' first recorded sermon, in the city of Nazareth, He included two Old Testament examples of God's heart for the Gentiles: Elijah's provision for a widow of Zarephath and Elisha's healing for Captain Naaman of Syria. Along with these examples, Jesus read a prophecy from Isaiah and then said, "Today this Scripture is fulfilled in your hearing" (Luke 4:21). He was claiming to be the Messiah—of both Jews and Gentiles—a concept totally contrary to Israel's preconceived ideas of nationalistic patriotism. For generations the Jewish people had longed for a Messiah to deliver them and bring them glory. It's no wonder that the people of Nazareth wanted to throw Jesus over that cliff!

Throughout His earthly ministry, Jesus revealed God's heart for all people. Yes, He was sent first to the lost sheep of Israel; but He also ministered to a Samaritan woman, healed a Roman centurion's servant, delivered a Gadarene demoniac, and fed four thousand people in a Gentile area. Even while on the cross, one of Jesus' final acts of ministry was to offer God's salvation to an undeserving thief.

Jesus taught with stories and analogies that conveyed God's love for the whole world. He called for laborers in the harvest. He commanded His disciples to launch deep and fish for men. He challenged His followers to welcome more guests to the wedding. Jesus told of a shepherd earnestly searching for a lost sheep, a woman stopping everything to look for a lost coin, and a father embracing a prodigal son.

Jesus said, "There will be more joy in heaven over one sinner who repents than over ninety-nine just persons who need no repentance" (Luke 15:7). If lost sinners matter *that much* to God and to the angels in heaven, they should matter to us.

Throughout the New Testament we see God's "scarlet cord" of salvation—from Philip preaching to the Samaritans and the Ethiopian in Acts 8, Peter bringing the gospel to Cornelius and his friends and family in Acts 10, in Paul's letters to churches comprised of both Jews and Gentiles, and concluding with John's end-time vision of "a great multitude which no one could number, of all nations, tribes, peoples, and tongues" worshiping together before the throne of God in heaven (Revelation 7:9).

Even in the map section in the back of most of our Bibles there are usually several pages highlighting early missionary journeys. It's not hard to find a biblical basis for world missions; it's hard *not* to see it.

THE GREAT COMMISSION IN EVERY GOSPEL

Jesus came and spoke to them, saying, "All authority has been given to Me in heaven and on earth. Go therefore and make disciples of all the nations, baptizing them in the name of the Father and of the Son and of the Holy Spirit."

Matthew 28:18-19

He said to them, "Go into all the world and preach the gospel to every creature."

Mark 16:15

He said to them, "Thus it is written, and thus it was necessary for the Christ to suffer and to rise from the dead the third day, and that repentance and remission of sins should be preached in His name to all nations, beginning at Jerusalem. And you are witnesses of these things."

Luke 24:46-48

Jesus said to them again, "Peace to you!
As the Father has sent Me, I also send you."

John 20:21

He said to them, "It is not for you to know times or seasons which the Father has put in His own authority. But you shall receive power when the Holy Spirit has come upon you; and you shall be witnesses to Me in Jerusalem, and in all Judea and Samaria, and to the end of the earth."

Acts 1:7-8

The Mission-Minded Child

Missions Theme	Reference	Bible Verse/Paraphrase
Since the time of Adam and Eve, all people have sinned and all need a Savior.	• Genesis 2:17 • Genesis 3:6 • Psalms 14:3 • Romans 5:12 • Romans 3:10	When you eat of its fruit, you will surely die. Eve ate its fruit; Adam ate it also. No one does good, not even one. Through one man sin entered the world. There is none righteous, no, not one.
From the beginning, God required innocent blood to be shed for the guilty.	• Revelation 13:8 • Genesis 3:21 • Leviticus 17:11 • Hebrews 9:22	"Lamb slain from the foundation of the world" God made garments of skin for Adam and Eve. It is the blood that makes atonement. Without shedding blood there is no forgiveness.
All people descend from Adam and Noah.	• Acts 17:26 • Genesis 10:32	From one man, Adam, God made every nation. From Noah's sons the nations spread over earth.
God is no respecter of persons.	• Romans 10:12 • Acts 10:34-35 • James 2:1-9	There is no distinction between Jew and Greek. God accepts men from any nation who fear Him. Be like God–don't show partiality.
God revealed His love for the Gentiles in the Old Testament Law and Passover.	• Exodus 12:48 • Leviticus 16:29 • Leviticus 19:10 • Leviticus 22:18 • Numbers 9:14 • Numbers 15:14	"Strangers" are invited to celebrate Passover. "Aliens" can participate in Day of Atonement. Leave fallen grapes for the poor and the alien. Strangers are permitted to offer sacrifices. Passover regulations for foreigners Sacrificial regulations for strangers
God promised that through Abraham and his descendants all families on earth would be blessed.	• Genesis 12:1-3 • Genesis 18:18 • Acts 3:25	In you all families of the earth will be blessed. All nations will be blessed through Abraham. In Abraham's seed all peoples will be blessed.
Through signs and wonders, many nations heard of God's power and gave Him honor and glory.	• Exodus 7:5 • Exodus 15:11-14 • Exodus 18:10-11 • 2 Kings 5:15	The Egyptians will know that I am the Lord. The nations will hear and tremble. "The Lord is greater than all gods" (Jethro) "There is no God except in Israel" (Naaman)
The Old Testament prophets revealed God's heart for all nations.	• Isaiah 45:22-23 • Jeremiah 1:5 • Jeremiah 16:19 • Ezekiel 39:21 • Daniel 2:28 • Joel 3:9-14 • Zechariah 8:20-23	Turn to Me and be saved, you ends of the earth! I ordained you a prophet to the nations. O Lord, the Gentiles shall come to You. I will display My glory among the nations. God has revealed the future to Nebuchadnezzar. Proclaim this among the nations . . . Many peoples and nations will seek the Lord.

Missions Theme	Reference	Bible Verse/Paraphrase
Notice God's love for all nations as expressed in the Psalms.	• Psalm 18:49 • Psalm 22:27 • Psalm 33:8,12 • Psalm 57:9 • Psalm 67 • Psalm 96:2-3 • Psalm 117	I will give thanks to You among the Gentiles. All the families of the nations will worship You. Let all the people of the world revere Him. I will praise You, O Lord, among the nations. Oh, let the nations be glad and sing for joy! Declare His glory among the nations. Praise the Lord, all you Gentiles.
God was glorified in the sight of other nations through Old Testament leaders and characters.	• Genesis 45:8 • Exodus 7:5 • I Kings 10:1-9 • Daniel 3:28 • Daniel 6:25-27	God lifted up Joseph before Pharaoh. God showed His power in Egypt through Moses. Queen of Sheba saw God's wisdom in Solomon. Example of Shadrach, Meshach, and Abednego All commanded to fear God because of Daniel.
Old Testament Gentiles who had faith in God were saved.	• Joshua 2:8-21 • Ruth 4; Matt. 1:5 • Jonah 4:2 • I Kings 17:7-24 • 2 Kings 5	Rahab, a sinful woman, is saved at Jericho. Ruth, a woman of Moab, joins Jesus' lineage. The wicked city of Nineveh is saved. God provides for a Gentile widow. Namaan, a Syrian captain, is healed of leprosy.
Through Jesus' birth, God proclaimed His salvation for all people.	• Matthew 2:1-12 • Luke 2:8-14 • Luke 2:25-32	Wise men from the East come to worship Jesus. "news of joy to all people" (angel to shepherds) "a light of revelation to the Gentiles" (Simeon)
Through His ministry and preaching, Jesus demonstrated God's heart for all people.	• Luke 4:25-27 • Luke 8:26-37 • John 4:1-26 • Matthew 8:5-13	Jesus' first sermon lauds two Gentiles. A Gentile man is set free from demons. Jesus offers a Samaritan woman "living water." Jesus affirms a Roman centurion's "great faith."
In His final words (recorded in all four Gospels and in Acts), Jesus gave us His Great Commission.	• Matthew 28:19 • Mark 16:15 • Luke 24:47 • John 20:21 • Acts 1:8	Go and make disciples of all the nations. Go into all the world and preach the gospel. Repentance will be preached to all nations. As the Father has sent Me, I also send you. You will be My witnesses to the end of the earth.

Missions Theme	Reference	Bible Verse/Paraphrase
When Jesus died, His blood was shed for all people on earth. Only through His blood can people be saved.	• John 1:12 • John 3:16 • John 1:29 • Colossians 1:19-20 • Revelation 5:9	"as many as received Him . . ." Whoever believes in Him shall not perish. "The Lamb who takes away the sin of the world" God has made peace through Christ's blood. You have redeemed us by your blood.
There is only one way to heaven: through salvation in Jesus Christ.	• John 14:6 • John 3:1-7 • John 3:18 • Acts 4:12	No one comes to the Father except through Me. You must be born again. He who does not believe is condemned already. No other name by which we must be saved.
Without Jesus, the heathen are lost, separated from God, and will spend eternity in hell.	• Romans 3:23 • Romans 6:23 • Romans 10:14-15 • Galations 5:19-21	All have sinned and fall short of God's glory. Wages of sin is death; gift of God is eternal life. How will they hear without a preacher? Those who live like this won't inherit kingdom.
God places in all people knowledge of God their Creator and a consciousness of sin, so that all are without excuse.	• Eccesiastes 3:11 • Psalm 19:1-3 • John 1:9 • Romans 1:18-20	God has put eternity in their hearts. "no speech or language where they aren't heard" "the true Light which gives light to every man" God's attributes are clear; we are without excuse.
It is God's desire for everyone to be saved.	• Ezekiel 33:11 • John 3:16 • John 3:17 • 2 Peter 3:9 • Romans 10:13	I take no pleasure in the death of the wicked. God so loved the world, He gave His only Son. God sent Jesus to save, not condemn, the world. The Lord is not wanting anyone to perish. Whoever calls on the Lord will be saved.
The early church believers were active in missionary work.	• Acts 8:4-6 • Acts 8:26-39 • Acts 10 • Acts 10:34-35 • Acts 16:9-10 • Romans 1:16	Philip went to preach in Samaria. God led Philip to an Ethiopian. God led Peter to Cornelius and fellow Gentiles. "I realize that God shows no partiality" (Peter) Paul's "Madedonian call" Paul preached salvation for Jew and Gentile.
In the Bible, the world is as a field "ripe for harvest." We must reap these souls now, before they are lost.	• Proverbs 10:5 • Joel 3:13-14 • Matthew 9:37-38 • Luke 10:2 • John 4:34-36	He who sleeps in harvest is a disgraceful son. Swing the sickle, for the harvest is ripe. The harvest is plentiful, but the laborers are few. Pray the Lord of the harvest to send out laborers. Look at the fields! They are ripe for harvest.
In Revelation, all tribes, tongues, peoples, and nations worship the Lamb.	• Revelation 5:9-10 • Revelation 7:9-10 • Revelation 14:6 • Revelation 21:24	"redeemed of every tribe, tongue, people, nation" "a great multitude from every nation, tribe . . ." "the eternal gospel to preach to every nation . . ." The nations will walk by its light.

CHAPTER 5

Our Historical Heritage

*"We speak God's wisdom in a mystery, the hidden wisdom,
which God predestined before the ages to our glory; the
wisdom which none of the rulers of this age has understood;
for if they had understood it, they would not have crucified the
Lord of glory." 1 Corinthians 2:7–8 (NASB)*

History is not just a random assortment of dry facts, dates, and wars. It's more than mandatory memorizations or an unending list of boring dead people. If viewed from a biblical perspective, history can become an adventurous mystery, full of God's eternal purposes and exciting action!

World history is the study of *real* people whom God loved—people with *real* feelings, desires, and dreams (much like ours) who simply lived in another time.

What is our purpose for studying history? As mission-minded parents and teachers, how can we incorporate a fervent heart for today's world into learning about the past? As we encourage our children in this area, we can instill an appreciation for God's amazing guidance, providence, and enduring love throughout time.

As your child considers an important historical moment, he or she can be challenged to make a positive difference in today's world. Timeless truths can be applied to present situations, and your child's character and thinking skills can be encouraged by asking specific questions. For example, you could ask your child:

- *What would it have been like to serve God as an Israelite in ancient Egypt?*

- *When Jesus was about your age, what was a typical day like?*

- *Did anything good happen because the early Christians were persecuted?*

- *What were some big challenges for early missionary pioneers in America?*

- *What would it have been like to travel across Africa with David Livingstone?*

As Christians, it's especially important to see the relationship between history and God's heart for our world. As you and your child look at a particular event, consider how the Lord was preparing the way for His future plan. Examine how people responded to God's call (if they had a chance to hear it). Focus your discussion on God's enduring love.

Ultimately, God orders the events of human history to accomplish His overall plans. Through every political change, God always remains the same.

No news shocks Him. No event alters His direction.

Just look at the correlation between these two "13:8" verses: Hebrews 13:8 tells us that "Jesus Christ is the same yesterday, today, and forever," and Revelation 13:8 speaks of Jesus as "the Lamb slain from the foundation of the world."

From the very beginning, God knew that Adam and Eve (and all of humanity) would sin and that the Son of God would have to die. Yet God still *chose* to create us and to save us.

But why?

That is one of the greatest mysteries of the Bible and human history. From our perspective, it doesn't add up; but somehow, from God's eternal and heavenly viewpoint, it made sense.

We need to realize that God was *never* obligated to create us or to save us—but He still did. And because of His amazing grace (and because of who He is), we owe Him everything. So when God gives us a glimpse of *His* purposes, or reveals an insight into a passion of *His* heart, we need to pay attention!

God's Secret Plan

Throughout the ages, God has always had a "secret plan" to provide people with access to a wonderful "endless treasure" He wants us to have.

For many generations, God kept His wonderful plan hidden from the devil. At the same time, He revealed insight about His plan to His *own* people—through sneak previews (prophecies) and secret clues (hints of God's plan)—so His treasure would be obviously recognized after it finally was revealed.

So what was God's "secret plan" and what is His "treasure" (and how does this relate to how we can help our child with history)?

God's highest prize (goal or treasure) for us is simply this: *knowing and loving God*—and being able to enter into a personal relationship with Him for all of eternity. In Philippians 3:14, Paul says, "I press toward the goal for the prize of the upward call of God in Christ Jesus"; and in verse 10 we see that this goal is to *"know Him* and the power of His resurrection" (emphasis mine).

Every historical event, every book of the Bible, and every God-purpose for people is connected to the critical moment when God's plan was carried out and His treasure was made available—at the death and resurrection of Jesus Christ.

God's strategy was incredible! At the cross, the devil thought he had finally outsmarted God. But in reality, God had totally outwitted the enemy, as the devil fell for God's ultimate trap! As Jesus died on the cross, His sacrifice paid the price for sin's penalty; and as Jesus rose from the dead, His triumph over death provided the way for all people to access His eternal life.

At the absolute center of human history is the cross of our Lord Jesus Christ. The cross is the transition point between the Old Testament and New Testament. It's the transition point in our dating system between BC (Before Christ) and AD (*anno Domini*, Latin for "In the year of our Lord"). It's the transition point in our own lives (as we respond to Christ's sacrifice) between our own spiritual death and God's eternal life!

 TEACHING OPPORTUNITY

Mission-Minded Overview of World History

"The Hidden Mystery of History" is a brief overview of world history from a mission-minded perspective.

As you read this outline, take time to *discuss* the questions with your child. I pray you will *discover* more of God's secret plan through time (the cross), *dig deeper* for more of God's treasure (a personal relationship with Him), and then begin to *distribute* God's mystery to others (by sharing the gospel).

The Hidden Mystery of History

To read aloud and discuss with your child

Do you know what a "mystery" is?

A mystery is a hidden secret someone is trying to find.

Like a detective looking for secret clues . . .

Or like an explorer hunting for buried treasure . . .

We're going to be searching for God's *hidden mystery of history.*

In the Bible, God tells us about a "mysterious plan" and an "endless treasure" that can help us to understand how all of world history works together to fulfill God's plans. Listen carefully for clues that point to God's plan.

> God himself revealed his secret plan to me. As you read what I have written, you will understand what I know about this plan regarding Christ. God did not reveal it to previous generations, but now he has revealed it by the Holy Spirit to his holy apostles and prophets.
>
> And this is the secret plan: The Gentiles have an equal share with the Jews in all the riches inherited by God's children. Both groups have believed the Good News, and both are part of the same body and enjoy together the promise of blessings through Christ Jesus. By God's special favor and mighty power, I have been given the wonderful privilege of serving him by spreading this Good News.
>
> Just think! Though I did nothing to deserve it, and though I am the least deserving Christian there is, I was chosen for this special joy of telling the Gentiles about the endless treasures available to them in Christ. I was chosen to explain to everyone this plan that God, the Creator of all things, had kept secret from the beginning.
>
> Ephesians 3:3–9 NLT

The Beginning of God's Story

The first four words of the Bible say, "In the beginning God . . . ."

In the very beginning, before there was any time and before there was any history, God—the Father, Son, and Holy Spirit—already existed.

God has *always* been around. He never had a start, and He will never have an end. God is *absolutely* powerful, He can do *anything* He wants, and He knows *everything* there is to know! God can be *anywhere* or *everywhere*, *whenever* He wants. He isn't limited in time (like we are): God has the ability to see the *entire* story of the universe in one glance. And God not only sees this story but is in charge of putting it all together; so all the details of history—or "His Story"—will turn out just the way He wants.

He is *completely* good, *totally* perfect, and *entirely* holy. And God is so full of love that He *is* love; and He is *absolutely* wonderful.

What are the first four words of the Bible and what do they tell us about God? ("In the beginning God . . ." teaches us that God has always existed!) Here are some big words to describe the amazing characteristics of God. Can you remember them? "Omnipotent" means all-powerful; "omnipresent" means being present everywhere at once; and "omniscient" means all-knowing.

The Beginning of Evil

Some may wonder, *Why then—if God is so good* (or *if there really is a God)—is there evil in the world? And where did the devil come from?*

God directs and rules the universe from a place called heaven, and He has an incredible throne surrounded by angels. Long ago a beautiful and powerful angel, named Lucifer, became so full of pride that he wanted all of heaven to worship *him* (instead of God). So Lucifer rebelled against God; but he was humiliated and cast from heaven (see Isaiah 14:12–15; Ezekiel 28:12–19).

Since then the devil (as Lucifer is now called) has been at work on the earth: trying to make God look bad, trying to tempt people to turn away from God's purposes, and trying to make God's heart sad by people doing evil.

Where did the devil come from and why is there evil in the world? (Originally, God created a beautiful angel named Lucifer, but he rebelled against God and became the devil.) What does John 10:10 tell us about the purposes of the "thief" (who has the same motives as the devil), and how does this compare to the purposes of Jesus? (The thief comes to steal, kill, and destroy; but Jesus comes to give life more abundantly!)

God's Design for People

All along, God has had a special purpose for people. As God's unique creation, people would be designed differently than the animals (or even the angels)—being made in God's own image (Genesis 1:27). People would be created to relate to God in a personal way and to work *with* God to help fulfill His plans. People would have an ability to create and make things, to enjoy beauty, to organize and plan, to imagine and dream. And very importantly, people would be created with a free will to choose whether or not they wanted to follow God's plans and purposes.

God knew it would be a very big risk to give people a free will. God could see into the future, so He knew way ahead of time that Adam and Eve would disobey Him and that all of their children and grandchildren and great-grandchildren (all of humanity) would inherit their sinful hearts. God could see all the evil, hatred, and selfishness that would come and separate people from His perfect holiness; and God definitely knew the very big cost He would have to pay (at the cross) to take care of this problem.

If God had wanted to, He *could* have designed people with preprogrammed minds that would only do what He wanted. But God didn't want people to be like mechanical robots or puppets. Instead, God wanted people to choose to love and serve Him by their own free will. God wanted a special relationship with people—like a relationship between a parent and a child or between best friends.

Because Jesus, the God-man, would be perfect, His life-giving death on the cross would be unlike any other death. The blood of Jesus would be able to remove the stain of sin from every person's heart, and the death of Jesus would be able to totally pay the punishment for sin that every person deserved. And then, Jesus would rise from the dead!

So God looked way into the future and saw all that would happen (including the cross and the resurrection and all the people who would someday be saved through His wonderful "secret plan")—and God *chose* to create our world.

According to the Bible, how are people different from animals and from angels? (People are created in God's own image, with a "spirit" that can relate to Him personally.) What does it mean to have a "free will," and why did God create people with the ability to disobey Him? (God didn't want people to be forced to follow Him; instead, God wanted people to love and serve Him by their own choice, or free will.)

The Ascension and the Great Commission

After His resurrection, Jesus appeared to His disciples many times during a period of forty days. At the end of this time, Jesus gave His Great Commission to "Go into all the world and preach the gospel" (Mark 16:15).

Then as Jesus ascended into heaven, He told His disciples, "You shall receive power when the Holy Spirit has come upon you; and you shall be witnesses to Me in Jerusalem, and in all Judea and Samaria, and to the end of the earth" (Acts 1:8).

A person's last words, or final instructions, are very important. What were Jesus' last words on this earth? What did Jesus say would be the purpose for the disciples receiving the power of the Holy Spirit? (To be a witness for Jesus throughout the earth.)

Persecution and Dispersion

During the time period of the early church, first the Jewish religious leaders and then the Roman government began to persecute Christians. If people believed in Jesus, they would get in trouble—perhaps being thrown in prison or even killed. But God used these bad things for His good purposes. Because of danger in Jerusalem the disciples started to flee to other areas, and the gospel began to spread.

In Acts chapter 8 we learn about Philip the evangelist. When persecution arose in Jerusalem, Philip went to Samaria to preach God's Good News. The entire city was filled with joy as multitudes received Jesus Christ. But then God told Philip to leave this mighty revival to go into the desert. There Philip preached to one important man—a government official from Ethiopia.

Do you see how God used this terrible persecution to begin spreading His Good News? (Because of persecution, the gospel went from Jerusalem to Samaria and, through the Ethiopian man, even to Africa. According to tradition, the apostle Thomas also took the gospel to India.)

Cornelius and the Call to the Gentiles (Acts 10)

The Jewish believers thought that God's plan of salvation was only for them, but God gave the apostle Peter a vision that explained His plan for the Gentiles. Peter saw a large sheet coming down from heaven, filled with all sorts of animals God had forbidden the Jews to eat in the Law of Moses. God said, "Rise, Peter; kill and eat."

Peter said, "Not so, Lord! For I have never eaten anything common or unclean."

This happened three times, and the Lord said, "What God has cleansed you must not call common."

Just when Peter was wondering what this vision meant, a messenger—sent by Cornelius, a Roman centurion who was known for being good and generous—arrived at the house where Peter was staying. An angel had told Cornelius to invite Peter to come and speak to him. So Peter went, and this Gentile man and his family and close friends became Christians.

Why was it so hard for the Jewish people to understand that God's Good News was also for the Gentiles? What did Peter's vision mean? (The Jews, who had always been God's "chosen people," did not understand that God's plan included non-Jews as well. Peter's vision meant that salvation was for everyone.)

The Holy Roman Empire

Oddly enough, it was actually when a Roman emperor named Constantine (who lived about three hundred years after Jesus) made Christianity not only legal but the *official and only religion* that history entered a period of time known for its spiritual darkness. God wanted people to have a free will to choose Him, but when the Holy Roman Empire tried to force everyone to become Christians, God's salvation message was distorted. Sometimes huge crowds were baptized all together—without a choice, and without even believing in God! "Christianity" and the "church" became tools for expanding a human empire, as religious leaders began using their power to gain money and military victory.

What can we learn from this time period? How does God want His gospel spread to others? (God uses difficult times to make us stronger. When the Christians were persecuted, they grew in numerical and spiritual strength; but when Christianity was forced on people, the message was confused. God wants us to choose to come to Him.)

The Dark Ages

The Middle Ages has often been referred to as the "Dark Ages." Only a few groups of monks and friars were allowed to read the Bible, they lived in isolated places called monasteries, and worship services were held in the Latin language (which most people couldn't understand). Religious Christianity was the center of this medieval age, but the true light of the gospel was so dim that it was nearly extinguished.

During this time, German barbarians and Viking invaders from the north came to conquer Europe; as a result, they were influenced by this "religious" Christianity, and knowledge of Jesus spread into northern Europe and Scandinavia. Through medieval art—largely sponsored by the church—many people learned about Jesus. (Even today, medieval paintings -which typically focus on Jesus and the Bible—fill museums throughout the world.)

Why was this time period spiritually "dark"? Was God's plan for people to have religious rituals or to have a personal relationship with Him? (Most people couldn't read God's Word for themselves, so they didn't understand God's plan. What God really wants is for us to have a personal relationship with Him.)

The Crusades and Holy Wars

During the "knights in shining armor" days, the church in Europe began the Great Crusades to try to win the land of Israel from the conquering Muslims (who had declared their own jihad, or holy war). Through the use of force the Christian religion began to spread, for a short time, into the Middle East. Other warriors used military force to try to convert the "heathen" in other areas to Christianity as well; but this type of Christian "expansion" left a negative effect on the world.

*Can you force people to become Christians? (When people are forced to become Christians, their belief is not sincere—you can't be saved just by **saying** you believe; you have to actually believe.)*

Early Catholic Missions

The Roman Catholic Church began to expand throughout the world (mostly for political purposes) into places such as India and Africa. During this time, God had a small group of people who continued to keep His Word and His truth alive. Through the missionary efforts of these people who loved God, such as Ulfilas, Boniface, Francis of Assisi, Francis Xavier, and others, many heard the message of Jesus.

Monks and Scripture

All through the Dark Ages, many monks worked diligently—all by themselves for many years—to protect and hand copy God's Holy Scriptures.

Many Christians were put in prison for their faith in Jesus Christ and some were even martyred (killed) for their beliefs. As Christians were brought to trial, religious leaders often heard powerful testimonies and God's message of salvation. Even though most of the religious leaders rejected this truth of salvation, God was still at work, and His kingdom could not be destroyed.

Can you see the "secret clues" of what God was doing during this hard time? How was God working behind the scenes to prepare for His Good News to spread? Why was it so important for the Word of God to be copied so diligently? (God used special people to make sure the Bible survived. They copied it carefully so that we can read the Bible just like it was written thousands of years ago!)

Reformation and the Printing Press

People began searching for knowledge and the truth both outside and inside the church, which led to the Renaissance and the Reformation (a time of spiritual awakening). As spiritual leaders such as Martin Luther and Ulrich Zwingli discovered the importance of salvation by faith, the light of God's Good News began to spread again. Through others such as John Calvin, people learned about the need for evangelism as the fire of the gospel began to spread.

With this new desire to "know things" came new discoveries and inventions, such as the printing press by Johann Gutenberg. The first book ever printed was the Holy Bible, and this invention of the printing press enabled the average person to have access to many books and teaching materials, especially God's Holy Word.

Can you imagine what it would have been like to hear God's Word for the very first time? How has God used the printing press to help spread His Good News? (Printing is much faster than copying by hand. Now more people can read the Bible for themselves.)

The Mongolian Empire

A mighty Asian leader, Genghis Khan, united the tribes of Mongolia and founded a kingdom that became the largest (geographically) in the entire world, stretching from northern China to eastern Europe and bordering Russia and Persia. During the golden years of this vast empire, the father of Marco Polo traveled to Mongolia and was able to share about Christianity with the great Kublai Khan. At that time, Khan requested of Polo, "Bring to me one hundred teachers of the Christian faith, able to show me that the law of Christ is best. If persuaded, I and all under my rule will become His followers."

Unfortunately, Polo found only two willing missionaries; and because of travel difficulties, they turned back . . . and Mongolia turned to the Buddhist religion.

The fact that no missionaries responded to this request was a missed opportunity in missions history; but God allowed this mighty Mongolian ruler at the height of his reign to hear the gospel of Jesus Christ! What lesson can we learn from this example? (God can help even the most important and powerful people in the world know about Him!)

Exploration and Evangelism

As people began to learn more, they gained an increased desire to explore and discover the world, as evidenced by famous explorers such as Christopher Columbus and Sir Francis Drake. Europeans began to travel across the ocean to faraway places in Latin America, India, and the Caribbean to trade with foreign lands. Stories about these distant lands began to spread across Europe. Christians came to realize the importance of sharing God's truth, and thus the gospel message began to spread.

As European countries started trading with other countries, many leaders in Europe began to establish permanent colonies in various areas. As European Christians traveled, their desire to spread God's gospel message to the unreached people in these faraway lands grew.

The colonial attitude was often bossy and controlling, but God worked through colonial efforts and early colonial missionaries to bring His message of truth and love to India, Africa, America, and Asia.

Do you see how God worked though people's natural curiosity and desires to learn about unknown places? How did God use empire expansion to spread the Good News of Jesus? (As people began to travel more, they carried the message about the Good News to people who had never heard about Christ.)

Great Missionary Heroes

Great missionaries began not only to *go*, but to *return* and excitedly share about the urgent need for foreign missions. Leaders such as William Carey, Hudson Taylor, and Amy Carmichael influenced many people—not only in "foreign" countries but also in their homelands, as many Christians finally began to understand the importance of Jesus' Great Commission.

How was God preparing the way for the future? Why did these missionaries take the time to share about the need for missions? (The missionaries knew how important it was to tell everyone in the world about Jesus. They wanted to get as many helpers as they could.)

Early Pioneers

In Canada, the United States, and Australia early pioneers began to move across their continents—to the west and to the interior. Some went because they wanted religious freedom or financial opportunity, while others were driven by adventure. Through these advances, the gospel began to spread to native tribes and to interior areas.

How did God use this attitude of adventure to spread the news of the cross? (As people reached further into unknown places, they met new kinds of people who also needed to hear about the Savior. This helped the Good News continue to spread.)

Nationalization

In recent years many countries have changed from being controlled by foreign colonial powers to being led by their own national governments. This switch has influenced the spread of Christianity! Now instead of just coming in and taking over, many missionaries focus on training local pastors, encouraging national churches, and developing national leadership.

Can God's Good News spread faster when more people are involved? (Yes!)

Specific Ministries and Multiplication

Across the world, specific global ministries are working together like never before. The *JESUS* film is available in nearly a thousand languages; Wycliffe Bible Translators is continuing to translate God's Word in unreached languages; YWAM and many youth ministries are mobilizing short-term and long-term mission teams; Missionary Aviation Fellowship is transporting ministers into remote areas; international evangelists are preaching to multitudes; children and orphans are being effectively sponsored; ministries like Samaritans Purse are assisting the poor; and missions books such as *Operation World* are helping us see the big picture.

As ministries have focused on specific areas, how has this helped God's secret plan to spread quicker? Why is it good for ministries to work together? (When we take care of someone's specific need, they are more ready to hear us share about Jesus. God wants all Christians to work together to help people in need and to share the Good News.)

New Advances for a New Generation

In recent years new advances have impacted our world in unprecedented ways. We can hop on a plane and fly across the world; we carry cell phones; we text message our friends; we send e-mails to the other side of the globe. We design international websites, access unlimited information on the Internet, and view live video footage from across the planet. All of these advances are merely tools that can help us take God's message of the cross to the nations.

Even now God is searching the earth for a new generation—to help write the final chapters of "His Story."

How can modern advances help spread the gospel to our generation? Can you see the clues of what God is doing on the earth today? (Computers, cell phones, and other modern inventions have helped us communicate better and given us a way to reach people who couldn't be reached without these inventions.)

The End . . .

How will "His Story" end? In the last book of the Bible, God describes an incredible scene in heaven where people from "all nations, tribes, peoples, and tongues" are worshiping the Lamb of God (Revelation 7:9–10). God's divide-and-conquer strategy is working, and the message of the cross will reach the ends of the earth.

We don't know how long "His Story" will continue; but we do know that Jesus said, "This gospel of the kingdom will be preached in all the world as a witness to all the nations, and then the end will come" (Matthew 24:14).

Reading these verses about heaven and the end times is like skipping ahead to the last page of a book and seeing how "His Story" ends. Will the message of the cross ultimately reach all people? (Yes!)

Conclusion:

Can you recognize God's *hidden mystery of history*?

- What was God's "secret plan"? (The cross.)

- What was God's purpose for the cross? (God wanted to give us His "endless treasure." Read John 3:16.)

- What is God's "endless treasure"? (*Knowing Jesus, understanding the power of His resurrection, and working with God to fulfill His purposes!*)

CHAPTER 6

Our Missionary Heroes

In each generation, God has called men and women to rise up and be "missionaries" for Him: to go into another culture or nation to share God's love. From yesterday's martyrs to today's global ministries, our heritage is great!

Many believers sacrificially gave of their lives so we could have the gospel, and now it is our turn. We have the honor and responsibility to convey this godly heritage to the next generation. We need to instill in our children an admiration for servants of God who lived for His purposes instead of their own.

🌐 TEACHING OPPORTUNITY

Mini Mission Biographies and Mission-Minded Monologue Skits

This chapter includes mini-biographies of many prominent mission-minded heroes. These brief summaries can serve as a quick missionary reference guide. Included are recommendations for great kid-friendly resources (to help introduce your child to the lives of these men and women of God), mission stories to read aloud, classic excerpts (primarily to challenge *you* to have a deeper passion for the lost), and ten enjoyable "Mission-Minded Monologue Skits" for your child, or someone else, to perform.

IGNATIUS

Early Christian martyr (AD 35–107)

Kid-Friendly Resources:

*   Christian Hall of Fame
    (www.Christianhof.org): Ignatius

*   Mission-Minded Monologue Skit (below)

Mission-Minded Monologue Skit #1

Costume: *Have Ignatius dressed in a simple Bible-time robe*

Setting: *Inside the catacombs, the underground tombs where early believers
worshiped (To create this setting, simply turn off all the lights and use
a lantern.)*

IGNATIUS: Welcome to this underground place called the catacombs. This is a secret place where we—as followers of Jesus Christ—can meet together. This dark meeting room is filled with tombs, but it is a safe place for us to come for worship and prayer.

My name is Ignatius, and I am a church leader (they call me a bishop) here in the city of Antioch. I like to encourage Christian believers to pray for people who do not yet know Jesus. One time, in a letter I sent to believers in another city called Ephesus, I wrote, "Pray ye without ceasing on behalf of other men. For there is in them hope of repentance, that they may attain to God."

I was born a few years after our Lord rose from the dead and ascended to heaven, so I never met Jesus in person; but John, one of our Lord's twelve apostles, was a close friend of mine. John was one of the three closest disciples of Jesus Christ (along with Peter and James); John saw Jesus glowing brightly on the Mount of Transfiguration; he was called "the disciple Jesus loved"; and he was the only disciple with our Lord on that terrible (but wonderful) day when Jesus died on the cross. John the apostle shared many of his personal experiences with me, and he helped me to know Jesus Christ for myself.

I have lived during a very frightening time, as Roman soldiers have often captured believers and put them in prison. And many of my close friends have been thrown to the lions and killed just because they believed in Jesus.

Even now my life is in danger. But I will always follow my Lord, Jesus Christ. In fact, *I would rather die for Christ than rule the whole earth.* I say, *Leave me to the beasts that I may by them be a partaker of God. Welcome nails and cross. Welcome broken bones and bruises. Welcome all diabolical torture, if I may but obtain the Lord Jesus Christ.*

NARRATOR: When Ignatius was seventy-two years old, he was thrown to the lions and eaten alive. He is an early Christian hero because of his love for the lost and his steadfast faith in our Lord Jesus Christ.

> "I would rather die for Christ than rule the whole earth."
>
> – IGNATIUS

POLYCARP

Last Christian leader to know the original apostles (AD 69–155)

Kid-Friendly Resources:

- Christian Hall of Fame (www. Christianhof.org): Polycarp

- Mission-Minded Monologue Skit (below)

Mission-Minded Monologue Skit #2

Costume: *Have Polycarp look like an old man with a long white beard and a Bible-time robe*

Setting: *Inside an old Roman prison*

POLYCARP: It has been over a hundred years since Jesus lived on the earth. Although I never saw our Lord in person, I was taught by the apostle John, and Ignatius was my friend.

Now I am a very old man, and I am known as the last individual on earth who personally talked with eyewitnesses of Jesus Christ.

I was born in the city of Smyrna, and later I became the bishop (or church leader) of this area. But I was arrested for my faith; and now I am condemned to die in a flaming fire. I know that soldiers will tell me to turn away from my faith in Jesus. But how could I do that? I say, *Eighty-six years have I served Him and He hath done me no wrong. How can I speak evil of my King who saved me?*

I remember the Old Testament story about Shadrach, Meshach, and Abed-Nego. They were threatened with the fiery furnace of King Nebuchadnezzar but were determined to stand firm for God—not knowing if God would deliver them or not. These three young Hebrew men were saved from that furnace. However, many of my friends also had great faith . . . yet they died and are now in heaven.

I do not know what will happen when they throw *me* into the fire. But no matter what, I am determined to stand in faith for my Lord Jesus, until the very end.

NARRATOR: Because of his steadfast commitment to his Lord, Jesus Christ, the old man Polycarp was thrown alive into a raging fire. According to tradition, his body would not burn—so soldiers killed Polycarp with a sword and then burned his body.

> "Eighty-six years have I served Him and He hath done me no wrong. How can I speak evil of my King who saved me?"
>
> POLYCARP

ULFILAS

Missionary to Gothic people (c. AD 311–381)
One of the earliest Bible translators (in the area of modern-day Romania)

Kid-Friendly Resource:

*   Mission-Minded Monologue Skit (below)

Mission-Minded Monologue Skit #3

Costume: *Have Ulfilas dressed in a simple priest-like robe*

Setting: *Ulfilas is sitting beside several old Bibles and many stacks of papers*

ULFILAS: Greetings! My name is Ulfilas, and I have been a Christian missionary for forty years among a barbarian Gothic tribe.

Let me tell you a little about myself. I was born nearly three hundred years after Jesus lived on the earth. My mother was from a Gothic tribe; and although my father was a Christian, he was captured by Gothic raiders. So when I was young, I did not know Jesus. Instead, I was raised in a very pagan, non-Christian home.

Thanks to God, I became a Christian and joined the church. In time I also became a minister, a priest in the church. After becoming a follower of Jesus, I began to have a great burden for the people who had captured my father. I left the Roman Empire to come to this remote tribe; and here

I have lived and conducted evangelistic work for forty years, sharing with people about Christianity.

It has not been easy. Throughout my ministry I have faced many hardships and much persecution. I am one of the very first people who ever translated the Bible into another native tongue, and it has been difficult work. I even had to develop my own alphabet for this unwritten Gothic language.

Right now the church and the government of Rome (the Holy Roman Empire) are one and the same, so Rome primarily sees my mission work as a way to expand the empire. But ever since I came to know the Lord Jesus Christ my heart's desire has been to expand God's kingdom—to translate His Word and to spread His Good News.

JOHN WYCLIFFE

Preacher and Bible translator (1320–1384)

Kid-Friendly Resources:

*   *John Wycliffe: Man of Courage* (By Faith Biography Series), Ambassador-Emerald International, 2004

*   See also Wycliffe Bible Translators (www.wycliffe.org), named in Wycliffe's honor

John Wycliffe was born in England and spent the first part of his life preaching the gospel to the poor and the lost instead of only to the wealthy in high places.

Wycliffe was once asked, "How must the Word of God be preached?"

He answered, "Appropriately, simply, directly, and from a devout, sincere heart."

Later in his life, the bishop (church leader) of London told Wycliffe that he could no longer preach openly about Jesus. So Wycliffe devoted his life to ministry through writing and Bible translation work. Today he is mainly remembered for translating the Holy Bible from Latin into English.

Thirty-one years after his death, the church protested Wycliffe's work by ordering all of his books to be burned. His bones were also dug up and burned, and his ashes were scattered on the Thames River.

Today, because of Wycliffe's sacrificial ministry, Wycliffe Bible Translators is named in his honor, and multitudes of missionaries are following his example and translating the Bible into many other languages.

MARTIN LUTHER

Leader of the Reformation (1483–1546)

Kid-Friendly Resources:

- "Martin Luther: Giant of the Reformation," in *Hero Tales*, Vol. 1, by Dave and Neta Jackson, Bethany House, 2005

- *Spy for the Night Riders: Martin Luther* (Trailblazer Books), by Dave and Neta Jackson, Bethany House, 1992

- *Martin Luther: The Great Reformer* (Heroes of the Faith Series), by Daniel Harmon, Barbour Publishing, 1995

Martin Luther is known as the "Great German Reformer" and a major leader of the Protestant Reformation.

As a Roman Catholic priest and monk, Luther worked hard to try to attain God's righteousness—even attempting to clean sin from his life through self-denial and self-torture. But after reading Romans 1:17, Luther discovered that the *only* way he could receive personal salvation and righteousness was by faith in Christ's sacrifice. From that time on, Luther began to recognize many wrong church practices, which he then condemned.

On October 31, 1517, Martin Luther attached a paper, called his "Ninety-Five Theses," to the door of the Castle Church in Wittenberg, Germany. This paper summarized major problems in the church, especially highlighting the practice of selling "indulgences" as a way of supposedly "buying" forgiveness. Luther was charged with heresy (teaching beliefs contrary to those held by the church) by the "diet" (or general assembly) that took place in the town of Worms. The emperor of the Holy Roman Empire, Charles V, issued the Edict of Worms, which was in effect a death warrant, though it was never carried out.

Later, Luther spent about twenty years translating the New Testament into German, as well as composing many beloved hymns, including "A Mighty Fortress Is Our God."

Martin Luther primarily taught that a person is justified by faith alone, every believer is a priest with direct access to God through Jesus Christ, and the Bible (not tradition) is the sole source of faith and authority for Christians.

Despite his great influence, Luther's theology was not faultless. His teachings against the Jews had a negative impact on many people throughout history. Also, Luther was so certain of Christ's return that he saw no need for missions and taught that the Great Commission was only for the New Testament apostles. (Later, the Lutheran Church realized the importance of international mission work and became an active force in world evangelism.)

Through Martin Luther's leadership, boldness, and influence, many people through history have been led to find true faith in Jesus Christ.

His life helped spread the true Christian message of faith throughout
Europe and the world.

"The just shall live by faith" (Romans 1:17).

MARTIN LUTHER'S THEME

COUNT ZINZENDORF

Founder of the Moravians (1700–1760)

Kid-Friendly Resource:

* *Count Zinzendorf: Firstfruit* (Christian
  Heroes: Then & Now Series), by Janet and
  Geoff Benge, YWAM Publishing, 2006

Nicolaus Ludwig von Zinzendorf was born into a wealthy German
family in the year 1700. As an adult, he once saw a painting of Christ
with a crown of thorns and the inscription, "All this I did for you; what
are you doing for Me?" Zinzendorf was greatly moved and proceeded
to found the Moravian Church, which became a worldwide missionary
movement that was unprecedented throughout the eighteenth century.

In 1727, the Moravians began a prayer vigil that continued,
uninterrupted, twenty-four hours a day, seven days a week, for over one
hundred years. As a result of this prayer movement—combined with
Moravian missionary evangelism—a tremendous revival began. The
Moravians helped spread Christianity throughout the world.

"All this I [Christ] did for you; what are you doing for Me?"

NICOLAUS ZINDENDORF'S INSPIRATION

DAVID BRAINERD

Evangelist to Native Americans (1718–1747)

Kid-Friendly Resources:

* *The Life and Diary of David Brainerd*,
  by Philip E. Howard, edited by Jonathan
  Edwards, Baker Books, 1989

* Wholesome Words website, Children's Corner, Missionary
  Heroes: "David Brainerd: Missionary to the Indians at
  Twenty-Four" (http://www.wholesomewords.org/children/
  heroes/hbrainerd.html)

David Brainerd grew up in Connecticut, in colonial America, as
one of nine children. His father died when he was eight years old and
his mother died when he was fourteen. Despite his difficult childhood,
Brainerd studied with an elderly minister, and in 1742 he was offered
missionary support by a Scottish mission society.

Brainerd began traveling to many Native American tribes but was
initially discouraged by their poor response. He eventually led his
national interpreter (and this man's wife) to Christ, and they began to
see tremendous ministry results. Throughout New Jersey, the Native
Americans were very open to Christianity and would often come from
miles away just to hear Brainerd preach.

During the summer of 1745 (during the time of the Great Awakening),
revival began to break out among Native Americans. As Brainerd shared

the gospel, he witnessed God's touch on their lives. "Many of them were then much affected, and appeared surprisingly tender," Brainerd testified, "so that a few words about their souls' concerns would cause the tears to flow freely, and produce many sobs and groans."

Brainerd had hoped to marry a woman named Jerusa, but he became sick with tuberculosis. Although Jerusa nursed him for nineteen months, Brainerd died before they could be married—at the young age of twenty-nine. The following Valentine's Day, Jerusa died of tuberculosis (which she had apparently contracted from him).

Although Brainerd's ministry lasted only five years, his mission work was significant to Native American people.

> "I would not have spent my life otherwise for the whole world."
>
> DAVID BRAINERD

GEORGE LIELE

America's first foreign missionary
(1752–1828)

Kid-Friendly Resource:

* Mission-Minded Monologue Skit (below)

Mission-Minded Monologue Skit #4

Costume: *Have Liele (with black hair and a beard) in a three-piece suit with a bow tie*

Setting: *In a tropical setting, perhaps next to a palm-like tree*

LIELE: It is God who brings freedom, and it is God who set me free to preach the gospel of Jesus Christ—first in America and then here in my new homeland of Jamaica.

I am George Liele. I was born in 1750 as an African slave in Virginia. My master was a Baptist minister, and he brought me to live in Georgia. There, when I was in my early twenties, I became a Christian and began preaching to my fellow slaves. My master saw my devotion to the Lord and my ability to explain the Scriptures, so he decided to free me to become a preacher.

I began preaching to other slaves in plantations along the Savannah River, and then I became the pastor of the First African Church in Savannah.

When the American Revolutionary War began in 1776, the British soldiers offered freedom to all slaves who would go to them for refuge. So when the British entered Georgia and captured our city of Savannah, most of my church members fled to them for freedom.

At the end of the war, thousands of these freed slaves were afraid they would be forced back into slavery; so many of them followed the British soldiers into Canada. I had led David George, a good friend of mine who was a former slave, to the Lord and trained him to have a fervent passion for missions. He fled to Canada and then traveled to West Africa to preach the gospel.

But I decided to sell myself as an indentured servant to a British colonel who was sailing to Jamaica. I had felt a calling to preach the gospel to the people here in this land, and this seemed to be God's way for my family and me to reach this island. We left thirty-three years before the Judson family left for India; so we were actually America's first foreign missionaries. The Judsons have the title, but God knows the truth.

I gave up my freedom for a time because I wanted to surrender to God's direction for my life. After I paid off my debt, I was again free to preach the gospel. I started a church here on the island—and from that, a Jamaican Baptist movement.

Yes, it is God who brings freedom; and true freedom only comes through total obedience to our Lord Jesus and His purposes.

NARRATOR: The church Liele founded in Jamaica continued to grow, often combining a zeal for spreading the gospel with expansion in education. By the 1840s, many Jamaican believers were sent to the African nation of Cameroon as missionaries.

WILLIAM CAREY

Missionary and Bible translator (1761–1834)

Kid-Friendly Resources:

*   *William Carey: Bearer of Good News* (Heroes for Young Readers Series), by Renée Meloche and Bryan Pollard, YWAM Publishing, 2002

*   *William Carey: Obliged to Go* (Christian Heroes: Then & Now Series), by Janet and Geoff Benge, YWAM Publishing, 1998

*   *William Carey: Father of Missions* (Heroes of the Faith Series), by Sam Wellman, Barbour, 1997

*   Wholesome Words website, Children's Corner, Missionary Heroes: "William Carey: The Consecrated Cobbler" (http://www.wholesomewords.org/children/heroes/hcarey.html)

William Carey is known as the "father of modern missions." He was born in England, and although his family was poor, he had a great desire for learning. By the age of twenty, young William had mastered five foreign languages: Dutch, French, Greek, Latin, and Hebrew. He became a minister; and from the very beginning he focused his preaching primarily on the importance of foreign missions.

When William Carey shared his burden for reaching the lost at a minister's meeting, he was reprimanded with these words, "Sit down, young man. When God sees fit to convert the heathen, He will do so of His own accord."

Despite this opposition, Carey believed strongly in the need to reach the lost and wrote a small book entitled *An Enquiry into the Obligations of Christians to Use Means for the Conversion of the Heathens*. Soon afterward, he preached a powerful message on missions. Using Isaiah 54:2–3 as his text, Carey challenged others to "Expect great things from God; attempt great things for God!"

Because of William Carey's leadership, an English missionary society was founded. Later, Carey traveled to India to serve in missionary work. During Carey's forty-two years of ministry, he and his coworkers translated the entire Bible into twenty-six languages and the New Testament (or parts of it) into twenty-five more. He developed several native language dictionaries and was actively involved in mission evangelism.

> "Expect great things from God;
> attempt great things for God."
>
> WILLIAM CAREY

 OUR OBLIGATION

An excerpt from William Carey's book on missions, in contemporary language:

Just as our blessed Lord has told us to pray for His will to be done on earth as it is in heaven, it is obvious that we should not just *talk* about that desire. We need to *take action* and do whatever we can—and to use every lawful method—to spread the knowledge of His name.

In order to do this, we must try to understand the spiritual condition of our world. This should be something we should want to do—not only because of the gospel of our Redeemer, but also because of our own feelings.

We often *feel* naturally "drawn" toward helping others and that is one of the strongest proofs that we *should*. God has given us His grace, and God has given us His heart and His spirit to care for those in need. We want to help other people because that is obviously the character of God.

DAVID LIVINGSTONE

Great missionary explorer (1813–1873)

Kid-Friendly Resources:

- *David Livingstone: Courageous Explorer* (Heroes for Young Readers Series), by Renée Meloche and Bryan Pollard, YWAM Publishing, 2004

- *David Livingstone: Africa's Trailblazers* (Christian Heroes: Then & Now Series), by Janet and Geoff Benge, YWAM Publishing, 1999

- Wholesome Words website, Children's Corner, Missionary Heroes: "David Livingstone: Over Thirty Years Missionary to Africa" (http://www.wholesomewords.org/children/heroes/hlivingston.html)

- *David Livingstone: Missionary to Africa* (By Faith Biography Series), Ambassador-Emerald International, 2004

- Mission-Minded Monologue Skit (see following page)

Mission-Minded Monologue Skit #5

Costume: Khaki clothes, a safari-style helmet, a dark mustache, a few props
(such as a rope over the shoulder, a machete, and a well-worn
journal), and an old-English accent

Setting: As Livingstone enters, it seems he is in the middle of an exploration,
slashing imaginary jungle leaves with his machete and breathing
hard.

LIVINGSTONE: Whew! Getting through this jungle is quite an
adventure—with so many valleys and mountains, fierce lions, and, ah
yes, those dreadful mosquitoes! But I tell you, "The mission of the
church is missions!"

I'm David Livingstone, and I have a heart for Africa. I'm a
missionary explorer, and I like to share the gospel of Jesus Christ,
especially in remote tribal areas.

It's actually quite remarkable that I could get all the way here,
since I was born into a humble family near Glasgow, Scotland. When
I was a boy I had to work in a textile mill from six o'clock in the
morning until eight o'clock at night. That was hard! But I was a
determined young lad. And do you know what I bought with my very
first paycheck? A Latin grammar book! You see, I wanted to learn all
about the world.

My family always went to church, and I was converted to Christ
during my youth. Then a preacher named Robert Moffat (who is now my
father-in-law) told me about his adventures in Africa. One time he said,
"On a clear morning, the smoke of a thousand villages could be seen
where the name of Christ had never been heard." That really challenged
me—so much so that I've spent my whole life traveling across the
interior of Africa, covering over fourteen thousand miles and one-third
of the continent! I've learned all kinds of things—about animals, plants,
places, and people—but most importantly I've been able to share with
unsaved people who had never heard of Jesus.

My life has been very difficult at times. I've been attacked by a lion; I've been sick; and people close to me have died. But I must keep sharing God's Good News of salvation, because *This generation can only reach this generation.*

And even now, I must *go*; and like I've written in my journal, I will go *anywhere, provided it be forward!*

> "The mission of the church is missions!"
> "Anywhere, provided it be forward!"
> "This generation can only reach this generation."
>
> DAVID LIVINGSTONE

📖 DID NOT YOUR FOREFATHERS KNOW?

A classic missions excerpt, from David Livingstone's journal

I was from the first struck by his intelligence, and by the special manner in which we felt drawn to each other. This remarkable man has not only embraced Christianity, but expounds its doctrine to his people. . . .

On the first occasion in which I ever attempted to hold a public religious service, Sechele (the tribal chief and a new convert) remarked that it was the custom of his nation to put questions when any new subject was brought before them. He then inquired if my forefathers knew of a future judgment.

I replied in the affirmative, and began to describe the scene of the Great White Throne, and Him who shall sit on it, from whose face the heaven and earth shall flee away.

"You startle me," he replied; "these words make all my bones to shake; I have no more strength in me; but my forefathers were living at the same time yours were, and how it is that they did not send them word about these terrible things sooner? They all passed away into darkness without knowing whither they were going. . . ."

HUDSON TAYLOR

Missionary to China (1832–1905)

Kid-Friendly Resources:

- *Hudson Taylor: Friend of China* (Heroes for Young Readers Series), by Renée Meloche and Bryan Pollard, YWAM Publishing, 2004

- *Hudson Taylor* (Men and Women of Faith Series), Bethany House, 1987

- *Hudson Taylor: Deep in the Heart of China* (Christian Heroes: Then & Now Series), by Janet and Geoff Benge, YWAM Publishing, 1998

- "Hudson Taylor: Englishman with a Pigtail," in *Hero Tales*, Vol. 1, by Dave and Neta Jackson, Bethany House, 2005

- *Shanghaied to China: Hudson Taylor* (Trailblazer Books), by Dave and Neta Jackson, Bethany House, 1993

- *Hudson Taylor: Founder, China Inland Mission* (Heroes of the Faith Series), by Vance Christie, Barbour Publishing, 2000

- Mission-Minded Monologue Skit (see following page)

- "Man of Mission—Man of Prayer," a classic missions excerpt (see following page)

Mission-Minded Monologue Skit #6

Costume: Oriental-style pajamas, round-rimmed eyeglasses, white hair, and a beard

Setting: As Taylor enters, he approaches a simple table with a candle, matches, a Bible, and an old-fashioned clock. He sits down, lights the candle, and opens the Bible.

TAYLOR: "Delight thyself in the Lord, and He shall give thee the desires of thine heart."

Yes, that Bible promise is true, as we focus and delight in the Lord—not in the ministry, not on the tremendous needs here in China, and not even on my exciting missionary experiences.

I'm Hudson Taylor, and I love to pray. Right now it is two o'clock in the morning; from this time until about four o'clock is my usual time to pray and study the Bible. During this early morning time, I'll be undisturbed as I wait upon God.

For many years I've ministered throughout China, because I believe *The Great Commission is not an option to consider, but a command to obey.* Sometimes my family and I have traveled with just a simple cart and wheelbarrow; sometimes we stay in the poorest of inns. But missions is so rewarding. Usually I eat, dress, and talk like the Chinese people; I've translated the Bible into the Ningpo dialect; and through our China Inland Mission, God has established over 200 mission stations, 800 missionaries, and 100,000 witnessing Christians.

And this is what I've always wanted to do.

Even when I was just five years old, I was known to say, "When I am a man, I mean to be a missionary and go to China." Back in England, my father was a minister who had always wanted to be a missionary to China. But when he couldn't go, he prayed that I, his son, would be able to go in his place. Growing up, I was weak and frail; but as a young man I wanted to come here so badly that I once said, "I feel I can not go on living unless I do something for China." And now, here I am!

But after all these years as a missionary in China, I've learned that my most important work is not translating the Bible, recruiting missionaries, or even converting Buddhists to Jesus Christ. Instead, my primary mission and calling is simply to pray.

I've found that maintaining a prayerful Bible study can be the hardest part of missionary work. I've often said, "Satan will always find you something to do, when you ought to be occupied about that, if it is only arranging a window blind." But when I spend time with the Lord, by His grace He fills me with His power and joy.

So now I will focus on this most-important work. I will "delight myself in my Lord"; and yes, "He will give me the desires of *His* heart."

> "I feel I can not go on living unless
> I do something for China."
> "The Great Commission is not an option to consider,
> but a command to obey."
>
> HUDSON TAYLOR

 ## MAN OF MISSION—MAN OF PRAYER

A classic missions excerpt, by Dr. and Mrs. Howard Taylor (Hudson Taylor's son)

God was first in Hudson Taylor's life—not the work, not the needs of China or of the Mission, not his own experiences.

It was not easy for Mr. Taylor to make time for prayer and Bible study, but he knew that it was vital. Well do the writers remember traveling with him month after month in northern China, with the poorest of inns at night. Often with only one large room they would screen off a corner for their father and another for themselves, with curtains of some sort; they then, after sleep at last had brought a measure of quiet, would hear a match struck and see the flicker of candlelight which told that Mr. Taylor, however weary, was poring over the little Bible in two volumes always at hand. From two to four in the morning was the time he usually gave to prayer; the time when he could be most sure of being undisturbed to wait upon God. That flicker of candlelight has meant more than all they have heard on secret prayer; it meant reality, not preaching but practice.

Because he did this, Hudson Taylor's life was full of joy and power, by the grace of God.

When over seventy years of age, Hudson Taylor paused, Bible in hand, as he said to one of his children, "I have just finished reading the Bible through today, for the fortieth time in forty years."

And he not only read It, he lived it.

AMY CARMICHAEL

Missionary to India (1867–1951)

Kid-Friendly Resources:

- *Amy Carmichael: Rescuing the Children* (Heroes for Young Readers Series), by Renée Meloche and Bryan Pollard, YWAM Publishing, 2002

- *Amy Carmichael: Rescuer of Precious Gems* (Christian Heroes: Then & Now Series), by Janet and Geoff Benge, YWAM Publishing, 1998

- "Amy Carmichael: Dohnavur Fellowship, India," in *Hero Tales*, Vol. 1, by Dave and Neta Jackson, Bethany House, 2005

- *The Hidden Jewel: Amy Carmichael* (Trailblazer Books), by Dave and Neta Jackson, Bethany House, 1992

- *Amy Carmichael: A Life Abandoned to God* (Heroes of the Faith Series), by Sam Wellman, Barbour Publishing, 1998

- Mission-Minded Monologue Skit (below)

Mission-Minded Monologue Skit #7

Costume: *Have a woman wear a long Victorian-style dress with a high collar and puffed sleeves, and with her hair pulled up loosely*

Setting: *Miss Carmichael walks in slowly, with very proper posture, toward a globe or a world map on a table. Have her point to the country of India as she begins. Ideally, she should speak with an Irish accent.*

CARMICHAEL: India. Yes, this faraway land is my home.

My name is Amy Carmichael, and for over fifty years I have been a missionary to the children of India. (Have her point to Ireland on the map.) I was born here in Northern Ireland. My family was quite wealthy. As the eldest of seven children, I had much responsibility—especially after my mother died when I was just eighteen years old. I helped my father a great deal, especially with the children.

In 1892, when I was twenty-four years old, the Lord called me to missions—specifically to India. It was not easy to travel back then. I went on a boat to Japan and Ceylon, came home for a brief time, then I set sail for this land of India.

This country is a strange place, so different from where I grew up. The streets are crowded with people and the air smells of smoke and burning incense. Most of the Indian people are Hindu, and they worship millions of idols and statues. They are so lost and so desperately need Jesus. In fact, the need in this land is so great that I have never returned home. So many of the children—especially little girls—were being abused in Hindu temples, and God has called me to rescue them. That is what I have done throughout my life. I have rescued hundreds of children, and I have worked hard to inspire others to come and help me.

I love to write; I often try to convey the need for missions to the people back in Europe.

One time I had a very vivid dream, which I wrote down. In this dream I heard tom-tom drums thumping all night as I stood on a grassy field next to a cliff that dropped down into infinite darkness. Then I saw people walking toward me and toward the horrible cliff. They were stone blind as they marched toward the cliff. I tried to warn the people, but no one could hear me. Though I strained, not a sound could come. Then, in my dream, my friends and family called me to come back home. They said they needed me for something important, so I went; but all we did back home was to sit peacefully on the grass and make daisy chains. One day, as I sat there in my dream, I thought I heard a cry of a little girl far away, falling off a cliff; but as I stood to go help her, my friends pulled my down. "You really must stay here with us and help us to finish our daisy chains," they told me. "It would be so selfish of you, if you made us finish this work alone."

As I woke up, I realized that God was speaking to me about the need to reach the lost with the gospel of Jesus Christ. And for all these years, I have stayed here in India to help as many people as possible, especially children. I continually pray, "Give me the love that leads the way . . . the passion that will burn like fire."

May God give us all more of His love for the lost.

> "Give me the love that leads the way . . .
> the passion that will burn like fire."
>
> AMY CARMICHAEL

MARY SLESSOR

Missionary to Africa (1848–1915)

Kid-Friendly Resources:

*   *Mary Slessor: Forward into Calabar*
    (Christian Heroes: Then & Now Series),
    by Janet and Geoff Benge, YWAM
    Publishing, 1999

*   *Mary Slessor: Queen of Calabar* (Heroes of the Faith Series),
    by Sam Wellman, Barbour Publishing, 1998

*   *Trial by Poison: Mary Slessor* (Trailblazer Books), by Dave
    and Neta Jackson, Bethany House, 1994

*   Wholesome Words website, Children's Corner,
    Missionary Heroes: "Mary Slessor: Mission Africa"
    (http://www.wholesomewords.org/children/bioslessorcc.html)

*   Mission-Minded Monologue Skit (below)

Mission-Minded Monologue Skit #8

Costume: Mary is barefoot. Her red hair is up in a messy bun, and she is dressed in
a simple African style with bright sheets wrapped around her.

Setting: She comes in and sits on the ground. If possible, have a few African-
style items, such as an African drum or some simple baskets.

SLESSOR: My name is Mary Slessor, and I will go anywhere for
Jesus.

While I was growing up, my mother instilled in my brother and me a big heart for world missions. She used to dream about my brother, John, becoming a missionary. But when I was twenty-five years old, something very sad happened: John died. Right then, even though I was young, I was determined to take my brother's place.

I had heard about David Livingstone and his adventures and explorations throughout Africa, so that's where I decided to go. Back then most single women missionaries only stayed at the established mission bases, where it was safe—but not me! My idea of missions was exciting adventure and exploration! I wanted to take the gospel to precious people in Africa who had never heard of Jesus. I've always been willing to go anywhere—even to places where the men couldn't survive!

I've always lived and dressed like the African people, but with my bare feet and native African clothing (and untamed red hair!), I've often been criticized. Some of the missionaries want me to wear fancy Victorian dresses, because they think my clothing is scandalous. But I just want to reach these African people, and I don't want my clothing to be a distraction to them.

It has been wonderful to serve the Lord as His missionary these many years. I've never been married or had children, but my life has been very full. I've traveled to remote villages. I've supervised schools and helped African children with their education. I've dispensed medicine and helped the poor. And most importantly, I've preached the gospel of Jesus Christ.

NARRATOR: After being called to Africa as a young woman, Mary Slessor spent the rest of her life in African as a missionary. She died in her simple mud hut. After her death, many missionaries (including those who had been critical of her) honored her as a great woman of God.

JOHN AND BETTY STAM

Martyred in China in 1934

Kid-Friendly Resources:

- "John and Betty Stam: They Lived—and Died—for Christ," in *Hero Tales*, Vol. 4, by Dave and Neta Jackson, Bethany House, 2006

- A missions prayer, by Betty Stam (see following page)

When John Stam attended a prayer meeting for missions at Moody Bible Institute, he met Betty, a daughter of missionaries in China. The two were attracted to each other, but their desire for marriage came second to their desire to obey God's call.

In the fall of 1931 Betty sailed for China, while John stayed for his final year of school. At his graduation, John spoke of advancing the Great Commission despite America's depressed economy: "Shall we beat a retreat and turn back from our high calling in Christ Jesus, or dare we advance at God's command, in the face of the impossible? Let us remind ourselves that the Great Commission was never qualified by clauses calling for advance only if funds were plentiful and no hardship or self-denial involved. . . . We are told to expect tribulation and even persecution, but with it victory in Christ."

After graduation, John also went to China. Betty went to Shanghai for medical reasons, and the two unexpectedly met. The surprise reunion led to an engagement, and soon the two were married. In 1934 they had a baby girl, Helen.

John and Betty worked with China Inland Mission (now Overseas Missionary Fellowship) and were assigned to an area where missionaries had been evacuated. Although assured of no "Communist danger" in the area, within a few weeks after their arrival John and Betty were captured, forced on a grueling march, and executed. A week later, little Helen was miraculously delivered in a rice basket across a mountain to the home of a missionary family. A Chinese evangelist had found the baby abandoned in a house about thirty hours after the execution.

The Stams' devotion and commitment to Jesus Christ still inspires people today.

A PRAYER

"Lord, I give up all my own plans and purposes,
All my own desires and hopes,
And accept Thy will for my life.
I give myself, my life, my all,
Utterly to Thee, to be Thine forever.
Fill me and seal me with Thy Holy Spirit.
Use me as Thou wilt,
Send me where Thou wilt,
Work out Thy whole will in my life
At any cost, now and forever."
—Betty Scott Stam

TEACHING OPPORTUNITY

Missions Challenge and Handwriting Exercise

Encourage your child to carefully read this prayer by Betty Stam and then copy it in his or her own handwriting. Your child may even want to write this prayer on the front page of a Bible. This prayer is a big commitment; but as we surrender our own plans and purposes, God can have His way in our lives—and God's ways are always best!

Did you know?

When Elisabeth Howard (Elisabeth Elliot) was only ten or eleven years old, she copied this prayer by Betty Scott Stam into her Bible and then signed her name. Elisabeth grew up to become a famous missionary and author.

GLADYS AYLWARD

Missionary to China (1902–1970)

Kid-Friendly Resources:

- *Gladys Aylward: The Adventure of a Lifetime* (Christian Heroes: Then & Now Series), by Janet and Geoff Benge, YWAM Publishing, 1998

- "Gladys Aylward: The Small Woman," in *Hero Tales*, Vol. 1, by Dave and Neta Jackson, Bethany House, 2005

- *Gladys Aylward: For the Children of China* (Heroes of the Faith Series), by Roy Lessin, Barbour Publishing, 2004

- *Gladys Aylward: Daring to Trust* (Heroes for Young Readers Series), by Renée Meloche and Bryan Pollard, YWAM Publishing, 2001

- *Flight of the Fugitives: Gladys Aylward* (Trailblazer Books), by Dave and Neta Jackson, Bethany House, 1994

- *The Inn of the Sixth Happiness:* a classic film, starring Ingrid Bergman

- "The Small Woman": a book excerpt, by Alan Burgess (below)

The story of Gladys Aylward is an inspiring missions testimony that appeals to both boys and girls. Even though she was small in size, rejected by a mission agency, and lacked money and education, Gladys was determined to obey God's call. Her adventure of faith and courage in China included stopping a prison riot, escaping a war-torn city, and rescuing hundreds of orphans.

For oral reading, I highly recommend *The Small Woman* by Alan Burgess; and for a heartwarming mission-minded movie, I recommend the classic film *The Inn of the Sixth Happiness*, starring Ingrid Bergman. (Though this movie is not totally accurate and Aylward was disappointed by a romantic scene that did not occur, it is a very inspirational film for the whole family.)

 THE SMALL WOMAN

A classic missions excerpt to read aloud, by Alan Burgess

Gladys Aylward was twenty-six when she made up her mind that more than anything in the world she wanted to be a missionary in China. Fortunately she was a very determined person; otherwise she could never have overcome all the difficulties that stood in her way.

She was working as a parlor maid in London at the time. How, out of her very small wages, was she going to earn enough money to pay for the frighteningly long journey to China? As she lacked the education to pass the examinations to become a missionary, she could expect no help in getting the money for her fare. She had to do it entirely on her own, but at last Gladys had saved up three pounds. With that in her pocket, she went to a travel agency.

The clerk there was amazed when Gladys told him what she wanted to do. He patiently explained to her that the cheapest route to China was overland through Russia to Tientsin via the Trans-Siberian Railway. It cost forty-seven pounds, ten shillings, but it was quite impossible to go that way because of the undeclared war between Russia and China.

"I couldn't really care about a silly old war," Gladys said. "It's the cheapest way, isn't it? Now if you'll book me a passage, you can have these three pounds on account and I'll pay you as much as I can every week." The clerk looked at her carefully. Then, defeated, he picked up the three pounds.

Gladys hardly knew what she would be able to do when she arrived in China without a penny in her pocket, and understanding not one word of the language. But she could at least learn to become a preacher.

"I must learn to talk to the people," she said to herself. So in every moment of spare time she went to Hyde Park, where she mounted a soapbox and preached, often to a jeering audience. Tired Londoners going home in the evenings were startled to find themselves being told to turn to God by a small girl, only five feet tall, in a black dress.

Then Gladys had her first piece of luck. From a friend she heard of Mrs. Jeannie Lawson. Mrs. Lawson was seventy-three, and still working as a missionary in China. She had written that she wanted a younger woman to carry on her work. When Gladys heard this, her mouth dropped open in astonishment, and she whispered weakly, "That's me! That's me!" She wrote to Mrs. Lawson at once: Could she join her in China?

Now it was tremendously important to save the money for the train ticket. In the house where she worked she was willing to do anything. She also besieged employment agencies, offering to work on her days off, and at night too, serving at banquets. Then came that wonderful morning when a letter bearing brightly colored Chinese stamps arrived. It told her that if she could manage to get to Tientsin, a messenger would guide her from there to Mrs. Lawson. The excitement! She would get her passport at once! She would soon make the money to finish paying for her ticket! "I'm going to China!" she said to all her friends.

JIM ELLIOT, PETE FLEMING, ED MCCULLY, NATE SAINT, AND ROGER YOUDERIAN

Missionaries martyred in Ecuador (1956)

Kid-Friendly Resources:

- *Jim Elliot: One Great Purpose* (Christian Heroes: Then & Now Series), by Janet and Geoff Benge, YWAM Publishing, 1999

- *Nate Saint: On a Wing and a Prayer* (Christian Heroes: Then & Now Series), by Janet and Geoff Benge, YWAM Publishing, 1998

- *Jim Elliot: A Light for God* (Heroes for Young Readers Series), by Renée Meloche and Bryan Pollard, YWAM Publishing, 2004

- *Nate Saint: Heavenbound* (Heroes for Young Readers Series), by Renée Meloche and Bryan Pollard, YWAM Publishing, 2001

- "Jim Elliot: A Modern Martyr for Stone-Age Indians," in *Hero Tales*, Vol. 2, by Dave and Neta Jackson, Bethany House, 1997

- *The Fate of the Yellow Woodbee* (Trailblazer Books), by Dave and Neta Jackson, Bethany House, 1997

- *End of the Spear* is a film that highlights these famous missionaries. It is too graphic for most children but is an excellent resource for teens and adults.

With Nate Saint as their MAF (Missionary Aviation Fellowship) pilot, five devoted young men—Nate, Jim Elliot, Pete Fleming, Ed McCully, and Roger Youderian—devised a plan, called "Operation Auca," to share the gospel of Jesus Christ with the Aucas, a remote and unreached tribe in Ecuador.

For several months the missionaries airlifted various gifts to these people, such as clothing, knives, and life-size pictures of themselves. On one occasion, the Aucas sent back a gift, including a live parrot and a smoked monkey. Because of this gesture, the men decided it was time to land. After one peaceful visit, the five missionaries landed together on the Auca's "Palm Beach." All five were brutally killed with wooden spears, leaving behind five young widows. *Time* and *Life* magazines both reported the incident; and although many believed it was a tragic waste of young lives, multitudes of Christians were (and continue to be) inspired by their sacrificial devotion to Christ and their desire to reach unreached people.

 ONLY THE GRACE OF GOD—SPEAR-WIELDING KILLER NOW CHURCH ELDER

An excerpt from *The Missions Addiction*, by David Shibley

Not long ago I met Mincaye, a member of the spear-wielding Huaorani (Auca) killing party who massacred Jim Elliot, Nate Saint, and three other gallant missionaries in 1956. Today, Steve Saint, Nate's son, lives with his family among the Huaorani. Mincaye is now an elder in the Huaorani church. And the man who killed Steve's dad is now referred to as "grandfather" by Steve's children. Only the grace of God can accomplish that.

Before thousands of evangelists at Amsterdam 2000, Mincaye gave this testimony:

"When I killed Steve's father, I didn't know better. No one told us that he had come to show us God's trail. My heart was black and sick in sin, but I heard [that] God sent His own Son, His blood dripping and dripping. He washed my heart clean. . . . Now I see you God-followers from all over [the world]. I see well my brothers and sisters that God's blood has washed your hearts, too. Go speak [about God] all over the world. Let's take many with us to God's place in heaven."

> "He is no fool who gives what he cannot keep to gain what he cannot lose."
>
> JIM ELLIOT

ELISABETH ELLIOT

Missionary and author (born 1926)

Kid-Friendly Resources:

- Elisabeth's Mission-Minded Family (see following page)

- For teen girls, I highly recommend Elisabeth Elliot's book *Passion and Purity* (Revell, 2002).

- See also the recommended resources for Jim Elliot above.

Elisabeth Howard was born in 1926 in Brussels, Belgium, where her parents served as missionaries. She attended Wheaton College and then became a missionary in Ecuador. After much prayer and seeking the Lord, in 1953 she married her former classmate, Jim Elliot. They worked together on translating the New Testament into the language of the Quichua Indians.

Jim and Elisabeth's daughter, Valerie, was born in 1955. Only ten months later, Jim was massacred while attempting to bring the gospel of Christ to the Huaorani people (known then as the Auca tribe).

Elisabeth has no regrets about the events that led to her husband's death, saying, "This was not a tragedy. God has a plan and a purpose in all things." Elisabeth continued to have a strong heart for the Auca people; so at the invitation of Rachel Saint, Elisabeth and four-year-old Valerie lived and ministered among these primitive people.

Together Elisabeth and Rachel worked to translate the Bible and to share God's message of salvation with the very people who had killed their loved ones. Their courage and love has inspired many in missionary work. Today Elisabeth Elliot is a highly respected woman of God. She was widowed a second time, and then married Lars Gren. Her daughter, Valerie Shepard, is a pastor's wife, a missionary in the Democratic Republic of Congo, and a homeschooling mother of eight. Elisabeth Elliot has written many outstanding books on missions, family life, and purity.

> "God has a plan and a purpose in all things."
>
> ELISABETH ELLIOT

 ELISABETH ELLIOT'S MISSION-MINDED FAMILY

Elisabeth Howard was raised as a mission-minded child. While growing up, her father, Philip E. Howard Jr., led the family in daily times of prayer, which included singing hymns together and reading the Bible.

Elisabeth's parents viewed hospitality as an issue of Christian obedience. They also believed that it benefited their family; for by opening their home their children could meet believers from different backgrounds, ask specific questions, and hear real-life testimonies of God's faithfulness. The family's hospitality (especially toward other missionaries) was often expected by their church; however, instead of feeling the weight of such an obligation, Elisabeth's mother, Katherine, told young mothers, "You don't understand what you're missing out on. You're missing out on some wonderful things!"

Of the six children in her mission-minded family, Elisabeth and four of her siblings became missionaries.

RACHEL SAINT

Bible translator (1914–1994)

Kid-Friendly Resource:

- *Rachel Saint: A Star in the Jungle* (Christian Heroes: Then & Now Series), by Janet and Geoff Benge, YWAM Publishing, 2005

- See also the recommended resources for Nate Saint above.

Rachel Saint was trained by Wycliffe Bible Translators and began her missions career in Peru. Later she helped her brother, Nate Saint, with his missions work in Ecuador. With the help of a young Huaorani (Auca) woman named Dayuma, she learned their language and began translating the Bible. After her brother and the other missionaries were tragically killed by the Huaorani people in 1956, Rachel began traveling and sharing about the mission need of this tribe. She spoke on television and shared at Madison Square Garden with Billy Graham.

At Dayuma's invitation, in 1959 both Rachel Saint and Elisabeth Elliot went to live among the people who had killed their loved ones, and they succeeded in evangelizing and planting a church among these people (which is still going strong). Over the years, Rachel Saint's name became nearly synonymous with "Bible translation," since she helped relay the importance of this ministry.

WILLIAM CAMERON TOWNSEND

Founder of Wycliffe Bible Translators (1896–1982)

Kid-Friendly Resources:

- *Cameron Townsend: Planting God's Word* (Heroes for Young Readers Series), by Renée Meloche and Bryan Pollard, YWAM Publishing, 2004

- *Cameron Townsend: Good News in Every Language* (Christian Heroes: Then & Now Series), by Janet and Geoff Benge, YWAM Publishing, 2000

- See Wycliffe Bible Translators at www.wycliffe.org

- Mission-Minded Monologue Skit (below)

Mission-Minded Monologue Skit #9

Costume: *Have Cam Townsend dressed in a simple 1920s suit and tie, with slicked-back hair and round wire-rimmed glasses*

Setting: *Sitting at a writing table with a stack of Bibles and many papers*

TOWNSEND: Hi! I'm Cameron Townsend, and I really love God's Word, the Holy Bible.

I grew up in a poor family in California; and when I was just a teenager I heard about the need for world missions. In 1917 I joined the

Student Volunteer Movement and headed to Latin America as a young missionary.

My first assignment was selling Spanish Bibles in remote areas in Guatemala, but I soon realized that many of the Cekchiquel people had no understanding of Spanish. I became deeply burdened for the hundreds of thousands of people who had no Bible translation of their own. (Could you imagine if the only Bible *you* had to read was written in a foreign language, like Russian or Japanese?) Well, as I was trying to distribute these Spanish Bibles, one of these Cekchiquel nationals asked me, "Why, if your God is so smart, hasn't He learned our language?"

Wow. I took that as a challenge.

For over fifty years I devoted my life to Bible translation work—personally translating the Bible, helping others to learn foreign languages, and motivating Christians to realize the importance of Bible translation. I founded a ministry called Wycliffe Bible Translators, which was named in honor of another missionary, John Wycliffe, who long ago translated the Bible into English and was killed because of his work.

The greatest missionary is the Bible in the mother tongue. It never needs a furlough, is never considered a foreigner.

Everyone should be able to have the Word of God in his or her own language, and that's why we need more Bible translators. Even today, there are still many people who have never heard of Jesus and whole people groups who do not yet have a Bible in their own language. We need to take that as a challenge. What are we going to do about it?

Please pray that God will continue to call people to work on translating the Bible into other languages. It's a lot of work, and the process takes a long, long time. But it's so necessary. And when you see your own Bible, realize what a blessing it is to be able to have God's Word in your own language. The Holy Bible is God's Word to us. We need to read it and study it. And we always need to remember to pray for people throughout the world who are still waiting for God's Good News in *their* language.

Well, I'd better get back to my translation work. Thanks so much for letting me share. Who knows, maybe *you* will someday help translate the Bible into a new language!

> "The greatest missionary is the Bible in the mother tongue. It never needs a furlough, is never considered a foreigner."
>
> CAMERON TOWNSEND

🌐 TEACHING OPPORTUNITY

Explore Bible Translation Work

Find a Bible verse written in a foreign language (search online or look in the front of a Gideon Bible, which has John 3:16 printed in many languages). Have your child attempt to write the foreign letters and words perfectly. Discuss with your child what it would be like if these strange letters and symbols were the only way you could ever read the Bible.

Check Wycliffe Bible Translators (www.wycliffe.org) for current statistics on languages that still need a translation of the Bible. (Wycliffe has many excellent missions resources available for children.) Pray with your child for God to provide missionaries and national ministers who can help meet this need, and for God to call children who can meet this need in the next generation.

ERIC LIDDELL

Olympic gold medalist and missionary to China (1902–1945)

Kid-Friendly Resources:

- *Eric Liddell: Something Greater Than Gold* (Christian Heroes: Then & Now Series), by Janet and Geoff Benge, YWAM Publishing, 2000

- "Eric Liddell: Olympic Champion and Missionary to China," in *Hero Tales*, Vol. 2, by Dave and Neta Jackson, Bethany House, 1997

- *Eric Liddell: Gold Medal Missionary* (Heroes of the Faith Series), by Ellen Caughey, Barbour Publishing, 2006

- *Chariots of Fire*, the popular 1981 film

- Mission-Minded Monologue Skit (below)

Mission-Minded Monologue Skit #10

Costume: *Liddell is wearing a plain white T-shirt and baggy white shorts, with black running shoes and no socks*

Setting: *Have Liddell looking at a medal or a trophy*

LIDDELL: Greetings! I am Eric Liddell, and I am a missionary here in China. I'm wearing my running clothes because in a few minutes I will lead some athletic events for the Chinese students at this school. I'm going to show these boys a few of my athletic medals, because I want them to listen to me share the gospel.

I was born in China, and this is where I lived until I was five years old. When I turned six, my brother and I were brought to England to attend a missionary boarding school; and my parents and sister, Jenny, went back to China. While I was growing up I only saw them a few times, just when they came to Scotland on furlough (to visit and to share about their work in China), but we loved each other very much.

I used to be known as the "Flying Scotsman," because during my years at school and at the University of Edinburgh I enjoyed playing rugby and running fast. When I was at the University of Edinburgh I became a champion athlete, and many newspapers said I was a potential Olympic winner. No one from my country had ever won a gold medal. Sometimes, because of athletics, I was chosen to speak to large crowds, and I enjoyed the opportunity to share about my faith in the Lord.

In 1924 I was selected to run in the Olympic Games in Paris. It was a tremendous honor to represent Scotland; but first of all, I was God's representative. When I learned that my qualifying race was going to be held on a Sunday, I had to make a very tough choice between running the race and following God's will for my life. I knew I couldn't run on the Lord's Day, which meant I had to surrender my Olympic dream. But God made a way: I was able to switch to a different race, and then God helped me win an Olympic gold medal!

Less than a year later I came here to China, where I've been working with my family and China Inland Mission. I teach and help with athletics at this school, and I serve as the Sunday school superintendent at the church where my father is the pastor. In 1934 I got married to a young woman, named Florence, from a Canadian missionary family and we now have three little girls.

The political situation between China and Japan is getting tense, so I don't know what is ahead for me. But no matter what happens, I will serve God and follow His will for my life.

NARRATOR: With the outbreak of World War II, the political situation in China became worse, so in 1941 Liddell sent his wife and children to Canada. Liddell was later arrested by the Japanese and sent to a prison camp. Even in this terrible camp, he continued to minister and help people—but food and medical supplies were very limited. Eric Liddell died in this prison camp, shortly before World War II ended. His sudden death brought shock and sadness to the Christian world, but his testimony has inspired many.

> "I know God made me for a purpose
> —for China. But He also made me fast;
> and when I run, I feel God's pleasure."
>
> ERIC LIDDELL, IN *CHARIOTS OF FIRE*

OSWALD J. SMITH

Missionary evangelist and spokesman (1889– 1986)

Kid-Friendly Resources:

* *The Challenge of Missions*, by Oswald J. Smith, Eternal Word Ministries, 2003 reprint edition (a missions classic for older children)

* "Dr. Duff's Appeal," an inspiring excerpt from *The Challenge of Missions*, by Oswald J. Smith (see following page)

At age sixteen Oswald J. Smith was saved at an evangelistic meeting, and he soon had a great burden for world missions. While still young Smith applied for missionary service, but he was turned down due to poor health since childhood. Longing to make an impact, Smith determined to start a missions-oriented church to send others throughout the world. He founded and served as the pastor of People's Church in Toronto, Ontario. This grew to become a large and influential congregation, sending missionaries and raising large amounts of funds for missions.

Smith's "faith promise" strategy enabled his church and many others to give multiplied millions of dollars to world missions. He established a ministry to northern Canada, a mission to reach Jewish people, and a gospel tract distribution outreach. Throughout his life (despite the warnings concerning his health) he traveled all around the globe as a mission evangelist, always returning home to inspire and encourage others. Oswald Smith is probably best known for his missions writings, including 1,200 poems and hymn lyrics (with over 200 of them set to music). His books include *The Passion for Souls* and the missions classic, *The Challenge of Missions*.

 ## DR. DUFF'S APPEAL

A classic missions excerpt to read aloud, from *The Challenge of Missions*, by Oswald J. Smith

Dr. Alexander Duff, that great veteran missionary to India, returned to Scotland to die, and as he stood before the General Assembly of the Presbyterian Church, he made his appeal, but there was no response. In the midst of his appeal he fainted and was carried off the platform. The doctor bent over him and examined his heart. Presently he opened his eyes.

"Where am I?" he cried. "Where am I?"

"Lie still," said the doctor. "You have had a heart attack. Lie still."

But in spite of the protests of the physician, the old warrior struggled to his feet, and, with the doctor on one side and the moderator of the assembly on the other side, he again mounted the steps of the pulpit platform, and, as he did so, the entire assembly rose to do him honor. Then, when they were seated, he continued his appeal. And this is what he said:

"When Queen Victoria calls for volunteers for India, hundreds of young men respond; but, when King Jesus calls, no one goes." Then he paused. There was silence. Again he spoke:

"Very well," he concluded, "then, aged though I am, I'll go back to India. I can lie down on the banks of the Ganges and I can die and thereby I can let the people of India know that there was one man in Scotland who loved them enough to give his life for them."

In a moment, young men all over the assembly sprang to their feet, crying, "I'll go! I'll go!" And after the old white-haired warrior had been laid to rest, these young men, having graduated, found their way to dark benighted India, there to labor as his substitutes for the Lord Jesus Christ.

My friend, will you go? Has God spoken to you? Have you heard His Call? Will you not answer, "Lord, here am I, send me"? And if you cannot go, will you not send a substitute? It is for you to decide. Why should anyone hear the Gospel twice before everyone has heard it once?"

"I have seen the Vision and for self I cannot live;
Life is less than worthless 'till my all I give."

"Why should anyone hear the Gospel twice
before everyone has heard it once?"

OSWALD J. SMITH

BILL BRIGHT

Founder of Campus Crusade for Christ
(1921–2003)

Kid-Friendly Resources:

* The *JESUS* film (available in over 900 languages)

* The *JESUS* film for Children

* "The Four Spiritual Laws"

* "Good News Comic Book" (a booklet for children)

* "The Man in the Clouds," a *JESUS* film story (see following page)

Throughout his life of ministry, Bill Bright was "fueled by his passion to present the love and claims of Jesus Christ to every living person on earth" (www.billbright.ccci.org/public). He founded and directed Campus Crusade for Christ, an interdenominational ministry, which has grown to become one of the largest Christian outreaches in the world—with 26,000 full-time staff members, over 225,000 trained volunteers, and ministry locations in 191 countries.

In 1947 Bill Bright received a vision from the Lord to produce a film on the life of Christ. He realized that a large majority of the world's unreached people were unable to read and considered how effective a movie about Jesus could be if it was created specifically to be translated into many different languages. Although he did not have the financial backing, Bright commissioned the *JESUS* film in 1979. God brought together producers, supporters, and professional people to make this dream a reality, including one couple who were willing to finance the entire original cost.

The result of this vision is the *JESUS* film, currently translated into over 900 languages. This ministry is directed by Paul Eshleman, who worked with Bright since the early development of this project. The *JESUS* film ministry has thousands of missionaries and national ministers working on this project throughout the world, not counting the multitudes of other ministries from all denominations that use this incredible tool. As of 2004, the *JESUS* film has been seen by over five billion people, with over 100 million people registering decisions for Christ!

Bill Bright also wrote "The Four Spiritual Laws," a gospel booklet used by many Christians and Bible-believing ministries throughout the world. This little booklet has been printed in 200 languages and distributed to over 2.5 billion people!

Did you know?

"The Four Spiritual Laws," written by Dr. Bill Bright, is available online in nearly every language (www.greatcom.org/laws/languages. html). This is an excellent resource, especially if you are sharing with someone who speaks a foreign language or are headed to an international restaurant and needing an appropriate witnessing tool. Also available online is Campus Crusade for Christ's "Good News Comic Book" for children (http://www.campuscrusade.com/Tracts_and_Booklets/good_ news_comic_book.htm).

 THE MAN IN THE CLOUDS

A testimony of The *JESUS* Film Project to read aloud
By Paul Eshleman, director of The *JESUS* Film Project

Several years ago in India, a young national missionary couple felt the call of God to take the gospel to a very resistant area in the north. They went with their three-year-old son to live among the Maltos people in a notorious area known as the "graveyard of missionaries."

They labored faithfully for many years without seeing a single person come to Christ. Their every effort to share the gospel was met with opposition. They battled discouragement, depression, spiritual oppression, and polluted water. Often, the entire family was ill.

One day the husband was returning home after seeing the doctor for his severe pain. As he walked through the door of their tiny home he collapsed and died. Distraught, his wife went to check on their sick child. He also had died. Devastated, confused, and with an acute sense of loss, she returned home, seemingly defeated.

A few weeks later, a *JESUS* film team arrived in that exact Maltos area. This time the government officials cooperated. The governor had previewed *JESUS* and instructed that the film be shown and not resisted.

Now, if you have seen *JESUS*, you know there is a moving scene when Jesus is first revealed at His baptism in the Jordan River. The moment Jesus' face appeared on the screen the crowd erupted with shouts and

exclamations. The team had no choice but to stop the film and learn what the commotion was about.

"It's Him, it's Him!" they shouted. They could not believe what they were all seeing. "He is the One we saw walking in the clouds!" The team was astonished at their testimony. It seemed that everyone had seen Him. It happened the day the national missionary and his son died. Clouds formed over the hillsides. The vision* of a man, larger-than-life, appeared above the clouds, walking over their hills, shedding tears. The Maltos people suspected that it was a message from God, that He was displeased that they had rejected the gospel.

Now, they were being given a second chance. They were stunned. As the team restarted the projector, the people settled down to continue watching the film. Everyone was transfixed by the story. Then, at the end, the majority of these hard, resistant Maltos people put their faith in Christ!

Other miracles followed. People were delivered from evil spirits. The sick were healed. The deep spiritual hunger of many was met. But the greater miracle is this: where once there were no Christians, there are now 46,000 Maltos believers and hundreds of growing and maturing churches! Today, they are preparing to send out their own missionaries to other unreached people, some of whom will use the *JESUS* film. The "graveyard of missionaries" has become the "vineyard of missionaries"!

** **Note by Eshleman:** For reasons we cannot understand, on occasion, the Holy Spirit breaks through spiritual strongholds via the use of visions. In this case, it appears that He affirmed the truth of the gospel contained in the JESUS film by allowing the man in the vision to resemble the appearance of the actor who played Jesus.*

 I PRAY AND I OBEY

A missions testimony from South Korea to read aloud

In 1936 a little boy named Yonggi Cho was born in the Asian country of Korea. At that time all of Korea was occupied by the nation of Japan, and most of the country (including Cho's family) followed the Buddhist religion.

As a child, Yonggi Cho became very sick with a disease called tuberculosis. His family thought he would die, but a Christian girl came and prayed for him and led him to become a Christian and follow Jesus. Miraculously, the little boy recovered.

When he was twenty-two years old, Cho started a simple "tent church" in the war-torn city of Seoul, South Korea. This church began to grow . . . and it has continued to grow. Today this church (Full Gospel Central Church), with over one million active members, is often referred to as the largest church in the world. God has impacted South Korea—through this church and many others—to such an extent that this country has become one of the greatest missionary-sending nations in the world.

Cho believes the success of his ministry is primarily the result of prayer. The church has a retreat center called Prayer Mountain, where people from around the world come to fast and pray twenty-four hours a day, on the strategic border of North and South Korea. Cho often says, "I pray and I obey."

According to Yonggi Cho, the most important purpose of church growth is world missions. This South Korean church has sent thousands of its members to begin "daughter churches" in other locations throughout Asia, in addition to thousands of missionaries throughout the world.

> "I pray and I obey."
>
> YONGGI CHO

LOREN CUNNINGHAM

Founder of Youth With a Mission (YWAM)
(born 1936)

Kid-Friendly Resources:

- YWAM and YWAM King's Kids
  (www.ywam.org)

- *Is That Really You, God?* (Loren Cunningham's
  autobiography), YWAM Publishing, 2001

- *Daring to Live on the Edge: The Adventure of Faith and
  Finances,* by Loren Cunningham, YWAM Publishing, 1992

- *Loren Cunningham: Into All the World* (Christian Heroes: Then & Now Series), by Janet and Geoff Benge, YWAM Publishing, 2004

As a young man, Loren Cunningham had a vision of "waves of young people" moving across the continents to proclaim the Good News of Jesus Christ. His mission plan was rejected by his denomination, but Cunningham stepped out in faith and founded Youth With a Mission (YWAM) as a nondenominational, international ministry.

Today YWAM is one of the largest mission organizations in the world—with over 7,000 missionaries in 106 countries. YWAM also established the University of the Nations, with campuses around the globe. YWAM's motto is "To know God and to make Him known," effectively combining short-term/high-impact missions with long-term missionary work (including evangelism, discipleship, and mercy ministries).

Loren Cunningham has personally traveled to every country in the entire world, and through YWAM he has provided missions opportunities for thousands of youth (and those "young in heart"). His life and ministry have greatly influenced world missions. Many give Cunningham the credit for "deregulating missions." He has helped open the door for many more people—of all ages—to participate in the Great Commission.

Are you interested in missions? Take a look at www.ywam.org:

- For children and their parents: King's Kids outreaches
- For young adults: DTS—Discipleship Training Schools
- For college students: University of the Nations
- For older adults and families: Crossroads DTS
- For every age: YWAM books

THE CHRISTIAN MAGNA CARTA

By Loren Cunningham

Everyone on earth has the right to:
1. Hear and understand the Gospel of Jesus Christ.
2. Have a Bible available in their own language.
3. Have a Christian fellowship available nearby, to be able to meet for fellowship regularly each week, and to have biblical teaching and worship with others in the Body of Christ.
4. Have a Christian education available for their children.
5. Have the basic necessities of life: food, water, clothing, shelter, and health care.
6. Lead a productive life of fulfillment spiritually, mentally, socially, emotionally, and physically.

A "BIG MAN" MEETS A "REAL MAN"

A mission challenge to read aloud
By Loren Cunningham

Paul Rader was a big, strapping football player who lived in the early part of the twentieth century. He became an imposing figure on Wall Street, where he headed City Service Oil Company. Then he got saved and obeyed God's call to preach, finding a post as an assistant pastor in Pittsburgh. Paul Rader would have

been appalled if someone had told him there were still false gods in his life.

One week, a visiting speaker came to his church. Paul took one look at the man—a missionary—and shook his head in disgust. First of all, the man was wearing a flimsy-looking suit of wrinkled brown silk. When he began to talk it was in a soft, delicate voice. He seemed a little frail. Not like a real man at all, thought Rader. As he spoke about his work in China, he often dabbed at the corners of his mouth with a handkerchief.

Paul approached the man after the meeting and challenged him. "Sir, why are you so sissified? You call yourself a man of God, but look at the way you're dressed and the way you talk. I don't think you're much of a missionary!"

The man patiently explained. "I'm sorry about this suit, but I have ministered in China for twenty-five years. When it was time to leave, all my western clothes had been worn out for years. The believers in my village pooled their resources to buy the silk to make me this suit, shirt and tie. They didn't have a machine, so they stitched it by hand."

He dabbed at this mouth again and Rader's disgust must have shown on his face, for the missionary continued.

"As for my voice . . . I did a lot of street preaching and was often beaten up. One time, a gang took turns beating me and a man jumped on my throat. My larynx is permanently damaged and I no longer have control of my salivary glands."

Embarrassed now, Rader murmured an apology and hastened to find a place alone. He went down to the church basement, found a pile of coal and stretched out on it face down. He cried out to God begging forgiveness for his attitude. He told the Lord he wanted to serve Him like this man.

From that day on, Paul Rader was a man with a missionary heart. As a pastor and leader in the Christian Missionary Alliance, he influenced many thousands of young men and women to give themselves for missions.

BILLY GRAHAM

International evangelist (born 1918)

Kid-Friendly Resources:

- *Billy Graham* (Men & Women of Faith Series), by Terry Whalin, Bethany House, 2002

- "Billy Graham: Evangelist to the World," in *Hero Tales*, Vol. 3, by Dave and Neta Jackson, Bethany House, 2005

- *Billy Graham: The Great Evangelist* (Heroes of the Faith Series), by Sam Wellman, Barbour Publishing, 2004

Billy Graham grew up on a dairy farm in Charlotte, North Carolina, and made a personal commitment to Christ at the age of sixteen during a revival meeting held by Mordecai Ham. "I do remember a great sense of burden that I was a sinner before God," says Graham. Later he learned that a businessman who helped plan these meetings had prayed for God to raise up a man from Charlotte to preach throughout the world. This businessman's prayers were definitely answered!

It's hard to talk about the life of Billy Graham without using numbers. He has likely preached the gospel to more people in live audiences than anyone else in history—to over 210 million people, it is estimated, in more than 185 countries and territories—with hundreds of millions more reached through television, video, film, and webcasts. As a result, multitudes of people have made personal decisions for Christ. He has preached in remote African villages and in the heart of New York City, to U.S. presidents and heads of state and to bushmen of Australia and wandering tribesmen of the Middle East.

Fifty times, Billy Graham has been listed by the Gallup organization as one of the ten most admired men in the world—by far the most appearances on the list since the poll began. He has written twenty-five books, including many bestsellers. His ministries include the weekly "Hour of Decision" radio broadcast, heard around the world for over fifty years, writing a weekly newspaper column called "My Answer," and publishing *Decision* magazine. Another ministry is World Wide Pictures, which has produced and distributed over 130 evangelistic films—translated into forty languages and viewed by over 250 million people worldwide.

Note: Billy Graham's concise salvation tract entitled *Peace with God* is a simple and excellent evangelistic tool.

"My one purpose in life is to help people find
a personal relationship with God,
which, I believe, comes through knowing Christ."

BILLY GRAHAM

FRANKLIN GRAHAM

*International relief worker and evangelist
(born 1952)*

Kid-Friendly Resources:

* Operation Christmas Child
  (www.samaritanspurse.org)

* Dare to Be a Daniel (D2BD) (www.daretobeadaniel.com): an excellent evangelism training program for young people on "How to Win Souls for God"

William Franklin Graham III is the fourth of Billy and Ruth Graham's five children. But just being the son of an internationally famous Christian evangelist was not enough. At the age of twenty-two, after a period of rebellion and world travel, Franklin Graham sat alone in a Jerusalem hotel room and totally committed his life to Jesus Christ.

Soon afterward, Graham was invited on a six-week mission trip to Asia by Bob Pierce, founder of Samaritan's Purse. During this time, he felt a call "to the slums of the streets and the ditches of the world" in areas affected by war, famine, disease, and natural disaster. Following Pierce's death, Graham became the president of Samaritan's Purse, a world relief ministry, which now provides more than $150 million each year in assistance in over one hundred countries—including an excellent missions program for children called Operation Christmas Child, in which shoebox gifts are sent to children in need.

Franklin Graham says, "Evangelistic preaching is what Daddy [Billy Graham] does; I never thought I would." Today he is the president and CEO of the Billy Graham Evangelistic Association and has committed to spend 10 percent of his time preaching and conducting at least five evangelistic festivals each year.

"Just being the son of Billy Graham won't
get me into heaven."

FRANKLIN GRAHAM

RON LUCE

Founder of Teen Mania Ministries

Kid-Friendly Resources:

- www.teenmania.com

- Global Expeditions (www.globalexpeditions.com)

- Extreme Camps (www.extremecamps.com)

Raised in a broken home, Ron Luce ran away from home at the age of fifteen and became involved in drug and alcohol abuse before finding Jesus at the age of sixteen. The life-transforming impact of Christ inspired him to dedicate his life to reaching young people. After graduating from Oral Roberts University, Ron and his wife, Katie, founded Teen Mania in 1986 with nothing more than a hatchback car and a dream to raise up an army of young people who would change the world.

Today Teen Mania Ministries greatly impacts America's youth. Throughout the year, Teen Mania's Acquire the Fire conferences pack stadiums across the country, inspiring crowds of young people to "Live God Loud!" and join the "Battle Cry" for today's generation. Multitudes are equipped through their Honor Academy and Center for Creative Media (located on the former campus of Keith Green's Last Days Ministries). Each summer, thousands of youth travel on Teen Mania's Global Expeditions. Through Teen Mania, over one million people around the world have come to know Jesus. For exciting opportunities see TeenMania.org.

"The Great Commission is
the Great Adventure of Christianity."

RON LUCE

LUIS PALAU

International evangelist from Argentina
(born 1934)

Kid-Friendly Resources:

* "Luis Palau: The Billy Graham of Latin
  America," in *Hero Tales*, Vol. 3, by Dave
  and Neta Jackson, Bethany House, 2005

* *Luis Palau: Evangelist to the World* (Heroes of the Faith
  Series), by Ellen Bascuti, Barbour Publishing, 2000

Luis Palau was born in Argentina and grew up in a Christian family. Deeply impressed by his father's faith as a child, Palau says, "One of my earliest memories is of sneaking out of bed early in the morning to watch my father kneel, pray and read the Bible before going to work." After his father's untimely death, Luis worked to support his family, and early in life he found his calling to preach the gospel.

At every opportunity Palau preached on street corners and shared the Good News of Jesus. He went to Portland, Oregon, to study the Bible and later returned to Latin America to build an evangelistic team. Palau began working with other evangelists, including Billy Graham; in the 1970s ministry invitations starting coming from Europe and other parts of the world. By the early 1980s Palau's ministry had made a great impact in Britain. In the 1990s Palau began to minister throughout the United States, at times speaking to crowds of half a million people. He has also ministered in the White House with national political and religious leaders.

Today Palau's focus is primarily on "festival evangelism": leading exciting contemporary city events including popular Christian music, exotic food stands, extreme sports skate parks, children's shows (cooperating with the popular Veggie Tales), and preaching—with no offerings taken from the massive crowds. Through his global outreaches, millions have committed their lives to Jesus Christ.

> "A nation will not be moved by timid methods."
>
> LUIS PALAU

RICHARD WURMBRAND

Founder of The Voice of the Martyrs
(1909–2001)

Kid-Friendly Resources:

- The Voice of the Martyrs website (www.persecution.com), which has many excellent missions resources for children

- dc Talk and The Voice of the Martyrs: *Jesus Freaks, Volume 1: Stories of Those Who Took a Stand for Jesus*; *Jesus Freaks, Volume 2: Stories of Revolutionaries Who Changed Their World*; Bethany House, 1999 and 2002 (an excellent resource for teens, adults, and mature children)

- *Richard Wurmbrand: Voice in the Dark*, by Carine MacKenzie, Christian Focus Publications, 1997

In 1945, a year after communists seized power in Romania, thousands of religious leaders gathered for a meeting at the parliament building. One by one, priests and ministers stood to praise communism and declare its unity with Christianity. Finally, Pastor Richard Wurmbrand boldly stood to speak the truth: "Delegates, it is our duty not to praise earthly powers that come and go, but to glorify God the Creator and Christ the Savior, who died for us on the cross."

From then on Wurmbrand was a marked man in the eyes of the communist government, and in 1948 he was captured and imprisoned by the secret police. He was brutally tortured, brainwashed, and placed in underground solitary confinement—separated from his family for a total of fifteen years. All the while, by God's grace he loved those who persecuted him, asking, "What can we do to win these men to Christ?"

Upon his release, Pastor Wurmbrand resumed his ministry among the underground church. After a government ransom was paid, the Wurmbrand family traveled to Scandinavia, Europe, and finally to the United States.

In 1967 Wurmbrand founded The Voice of the Martyrs, a ministry dedicated to serving the persecuted church worldwide and seeing freedoms won in places that persecute Christianity (see www.persecution.com).

> "What can we do to win these men to Christ?"
>
> RICHARD WURMBRAND, SPEAKING OF THE MEN
> PERSECUTING HIM

K. P. YOHANNAN

Founder of Gospel for Asia

Kid-Friendly Resource:

* *Revolution in World Missions*, by K. P. Yohannan (available free at www.gfa.org or by calling 1-800-WIN-ASIA)

K. P. Yohannan grew up in a very poor family in India, but today he directs a large international ministry, Gospel for Asia. This far-reaching mission outreach supports over eleven thousand full-time national missionaries throughout Asia. With ministry training centers throughout India and thousands of current students, Gospel for Asia is one of the most powerful missionary movements working across the nation of India in evangelism and church planting.

Every year, Gospel for Asia produces nearly 50 million pieces of gospel literature to supply national missionaries as they preach the gospel and win people to Christ. More than 14,000 fellowships and more than 3,230 fully established churches have been planted. Other ministry areas include radio and film outreach, ministry to Muslims, ministry in slums, and providing national missionaries with vehicles and ministry tools.

In his exciting and fast-moving book, *Revolution in World Missions*, Yohannan shares how God brought him from his remote Indian village to become the founder of Gospel for Asia.

"Walk away from your own preoccupations to the harvest fields of Asia—and see the perishing multitudes through the eyes of Jesus."

K. P. YOHANNAN

God Can Use Anyone—Including YOU!

Around the world today, God is working mightily through willing individuals. Some missionaries are getting older, but others are young, daring, and full of adventure . . . some missionaries are even little children! Some have fair skin, but multitudes of today's missionaries have dark-colored skin. Some missionaries travel around the world on commercial airline jets or small Missionary Aviation Fellowship bush planes, but many travel by motorcycle, or bicycle, or even on foot. Some are well-known and even famous.

One day when we get to heaven, we will have the opportunity to meet all of God's unknown heroes. Just because we've never heard of them doesn't mean they're not important! God is the One who rewards all His true "missionary heroes." He sees everything, and He is searching for faithful followers who will fulfill the special and unique mission He has planned for their lives—whatever that calling may be—whether or not anyone ever hears about them or ever acknowledges what they do.

This final mission testimony is a special tribute to the multitudes of national missionaries throughout the world.

DRAKE AND JOSEPHINE KANAABO

National evangelists with Harvest Ministry

Drake Kanaabo was one of many children born on the mud floor of a humble village home. His Muslim father had several wives, but the family was so poor that Drake did not even have a pair of shoes until he was sixteen years old!

As a young man, Drake's only dream was merely to survive, since Idi Amin, a brutal dictator, ruled his war-torn country of Uganda. One day Amin's soldiers attacked Drake's village and began killing all the men. Drake fled for his life and took refuge in a room where Christian women were fervently praying. One woman felt the Lord tell her that no one in the room would die. The next morning Drake discovered that every other man in the village had been murdered. Right away he went back and asked the women to help him pray to receive Jesus Christ.

From then on, Drake Kanaabo had a new "dream" for his life. More than anything, he wanted to share this Good News he had found. But he lived in terrible poverty and had only a meager job repairing old radios. Could God ever use him? For many years Drake was simply faithful—loving the Lord and boldly preaching whenever he could.

His young wife, Josephine, also came to Jesus; but she was shy and desperate for God to answer her deepest prayer. Year after year Drake and Josephine had prayed for a child, but Josephine had been unable to have a baby. Unsaved family members and neighbors in their village often mocked them and encouraged Drake to "chase his wife away" and get a new one who could give him children. But Drake and Josephine refused to give up. Finally, after fifteen years, the Kanaabos had two boys, Samuel and John.

Today Drake Kanaabo is an international evangelist, and he and Josephine are two of our dearest friends. Since 1991 God has provided the way for Drake to proclaim the Good News of Jesus Christ throughout his country of Uganda and around the world. He has preached across the continent of Africa, throughout Europe, across the United States and the Middle East, into India, and on remote islands of Asia. He enjoys preaching to crowds of up to seventy thousand people—and to individuals, one-to-one.

Along with raising their children, Josephine helps direct Harvest Ministry's "Osanidde Village" orphanage, and she encourages African women. No longer shy and timid, Josephine now boldly shares the gospel of Jesus Christ with huge crowds.

* * *

When this book was nearly completed, Drake Kanaabo was given an all-expense-paid trip to Israel. Right as I was finishing this missions hero chapter, Drake sent us an exciting message from Jerusalem, the very place where world missions began. Our African friend had just led a Western tourist to Jesus Christ—inside of the Garden Tomb!

This is why we have a heart for missions. The tomb of Jesus Christ is empty and our True Hero is alive!

Even now, God is searching the whole earth—not for the "mighty and talented," but for the "humble and obedient" of all ages who will simply work *with Him* to share His Good News.

PART III

Our Mission-Minded Focus

CHAPTER 7

Training Your Child in Biblical Christianity

We need to train ourselves and our children in the important foundations of our faith. This chapter can be used as a reference tool to help effectively train a new generation to be "rock solid" for Jesus Christ. Never underestimate the ability of your child to learn God's Word! As your child matures, he or she will build upon the early foundational training received. Even a little child can be well-grounded in sound biblical doctrine and well-established in a meaningful relationship with the Lord.

TEACHING OPPORTUNITY

Foundational Bible Verses to Memorize

Share the gospel with your child—and teach your child to share it! Go through these basic foundations of faith with your child, and make sure he or she understands what it means to be saved and how to share the gospel with others. Encourage your child to check off each verse as he or she memorizes it.

One of life's greatest privileges is being able to lead a child into a genuine, personal relationship with Jesus Christ. I always want to remember to keep this focus, because every child will someday stand before God. As parents and teachers, our number one priority should be to make certain that each child we are influencing has an opportunity to receive Jesus Christ as his or her personal Lord and Savior.

Q. What does it mean to be "saved"?

Many people who call themselves "Christians" (including many children) have no understanding of what it really means to be saved. Just because someone is a basically good person does not mean that he or she is in right standing with God and will someday go to heaven. The Bible teaches us that people cannot get to heaven merely by being good, by being born into a religious family, or even by believing there is a God (in James 2:19, the Bible says, "You believe that there is one God. You do well. Even the demons believe—and tremble!").

Q. How are we saved, or "born again"?

There is only one way to be saved and that is through receiving God's salvation through Jesus Christ—by being "born again." We were each born the first time, physically, as a baby; but we must also be born a second time, born again spiritually. God's salvation is by grace (a gift we don't deserve and haven't earned), through faith in Jesus Christ.

Jesus was the first person to use the term "born again" when he said:

❑   John 3:7   "You must be born again."

❑   John 3:3   "Unless one is born again, he cannot see the kingdom of God."

Q. What is sin?

Sin is anything a person does (or neglects to do) that falls short of God's perfect will and His perfect law. Like missing a target, sin is missing God's will for our lives. As a person comes to Jesus Christ, he or she must repent (or turn away) from all sin.

❑   Romans 3:23   "For all have sinned and fall short of the glory of God."

Q. Is there really only one way to God?

Yes! There is only one way a person can receive God's eternal life and that is through God's salvation by His grace that we receive by faith in Jesus Christ! The Bible says:

❑ John 14:6   "Jesus said to him, 'I am the way, the truth, and the life. No one comes to the Father except through Me.'"

❑ Acts 4:12   "Nor is there salvation in any other, for there is no other name under heaven given among men by which we must be saved."

Q. Why do we need God's salvation?

If you were to die right now, do you know without a doubt that you would go to heaven—and how do you know? Someday, when you die, you will stand face-to-face with the perfect, holy, almighty God, and you will be judged (see Hebrews 9:27). God has undeniable evidence of every wrong thing you have ever done and of every bad thought you have ever imagined. On that day there will be no excuses and no way to hide. If you are trusting in yourself, you will be pronounced guilty of sin and of not measuring up to God's perfect law, and not even following the conviction of your own conscience (what you know in your heart is the right thing to do). It will not matter if your sins are many or few, or how many "good things" you did. On God's day of judgment our only hope will be to know that we have received God's salvation and cleansing from sin through the death of Jesus Christ on the cross.

❑ 1 Peter 2:24   "He Himself bore our sins in His body on the cross, so that we might die to sin and live to righteousness; for by His wounds you were healed" (NASB).

Q. How can we know for sure if we're really saved and going to heaven?

We can have assurance (or "know for sure") about our salvation from what God has told us in the Bible. Our salvation is not based on our feelings but on the fact of God's Word.

❑   1 John 5:11–13 "And this is the testimony: that God has given us eternal life, and this life is in His Son. He who has the Son has life; he who does not have the Son of God does not have life. These things I have written to you who believe in the name of the Son of God; that you may know that you have eternal life, and that you may continue to believe in the name of the Son of God."

Q. How can we receive Jesus Christ?

After you hear and understand God's plan of salvation, you must accept and believe it for yourself, and then confess your sins to God and confess Jesus Christ as the Lord and Savior of your life.

It's as simple to remember as A, B, C: Accept, Believe, and Confess!

A—Accept: God loves you and has a purpose for your life.

❑   John 3:16   "For God so loved the world that He gave His only begotten Son, that whoever believes in Him should not perish but have everlasting life."

B—Believe: Jesus Christ is God's only provision for our sin.

❑   Romans 6:23   "For the wages of sin is death, but the gift of God is eternal life in Christ Jesus our Lord."

Each person must individually receive God's salvation through faith in Jesus Christ. Our salvation is a gift of God's grace.

❏ Ephesians 2:8   "For by grace you have been saved through faith, and that not of yourselves; it is the gift of God."

C—Confess: Completely surrender your life to Jesus Christ! Confess your sins to God, and confess (speak out of your mouth) that Jesus is your Lord and Savior.

❏ Romans 10:9–10   "If you confess with your mouth that Jesus is Lord and believe in your heart that God raised him from the dead, you will be saved. For it is by believing in your heart that you are made right with God, and it is by confessing with your mouth that you are saved" (NLT).

Q. What is an example of a "sinner's prayer"?

The following prayer is an example of a simple prayer to receive Jesus Christ as the Lord and Savior of your life. This type of prayer is often called a "sinner's prayer" because it is a prayer of turning away from sin to receive God's salvation. Your prayer does not have to use these exact words, because God knows your heart. But when praying to receive Jesus Christ as your Lord and Savior, it's good to speak your prayer out loud—"confessing" (or saying) it with your mouth.

Dear Heavenly Father,

I know that I have sinned, and I know that my sin would keep me from You forever. But I thank You, God, for sending Your Son, Jesus Christ, to die on the cross for me and to pay this price for my sins. I don't deserve Your gift of salvation, but I am now turning away from the wrong things I have done and I receive Your Son, Jesus Christ, as my Lord and Savior. Jesus, You are now my Lord! Please come into my life and forgive all my sins. I believe that You are alive, and I thank You for giving me Your new life. Help me live for You all the days of my life. I love You, Lord, and give my entire life to You.

In Jesus' name, Amen.

Name: _____

Date: _____

❑   2 Corinthians 6:2   "Behold, now is the accepted time; behold, now is the day of salvation."

Q. What is the Bible all about?

The Bible is the most remarkable book ever written. It is a God-inspired library of sixty-six books—both large and small—including history, poetry, psalms (hymns or songs), letters, teachings, and proverbs (wise sayings). The Bible contains the deepest wisdom and knowledge, yet it is simple enough for a child to understand. The Holy Bible is divided into two main sections:

- **The Old Testament** contains thirty-nine books and was written before the birth of Jesus Christ. It tells of the creation of the world and the fall of humanity through sin, and it contains many prophecies concerning the birth, life, death, and resurrection of the promised Messiah (Jesus Christ). The Old Testament shows us how people could never meet all the perfect requirements of God's law and how we all desperately need a Savior.

- **The New Testament** contains twenty-seven books and was written after the resurrection of Jesus Christ. The first four books, the Gospels, give the history of Christ's life and ministry. The book of Acts tells how Jesus' disciples carried on the work of Christ and how Christianity began. Most of the remaining New Testament books give practical instructions for Christian living and instructions for the church. The final book, Revelation, is a prophetic book, telling us about the end times and the second coming of our Lord Jesus.

Q. How can I know the Bible is true?

- God's Word is alive and life-changing!

  The Bible is never out-of-date on any subject, and its teachings fulfill the spiritual and moral needs of all people, young and old, in all lands, and in any time period. Over and over (some say 3,800 times) the Bible claims to be the actual Word of God; for example, 2 Timothy 3:16 says, "All Scripture is inspired by God and is useful to teach us what is true and to make us realize what is wrong in our lives. It corrects us when we are wrong and teaches us to do what is right" (NLT).

- God's Word fits together like a perfect puzzle!

  Approximately forty writers—all directed and supernaturally led by God—wrote the sixty-six books of the Bible over a period of about sixteen hundred years. These writers lived in many different lands and were from a wide range of social classes: from kings and scholars to prophets, fishermen, and shepherds. Many writers never saw the words of the others, yet the books of the Bible are all totally true and never stray from the Bible's central message of salvation through the promised Savior and Messiah—our Lord, Jesus Christ!

- God's Word is totally accurate!

  The Bible is scientifically accurate and historically correct. Its truths have withstood the test of time, as many biblical details have been proven to be true through archeological discoveries, through factual research in the areas of botany, geology, and astronomy, and through studies of ancient history.

- The prophecies of God's Word come true!

  The Bible contains over five thousand prophecies, many of which were predicted hundreds or even thousands of years before their fulfillment. Most of the prophecies of the Bible have already been completely fulfilled; the rest are being fulfilled now or will be fulfilled in times to come.

- God's Word has changed and impacted the world!

  The Bible has blessed millions of people from generation to generation. Throughout the ages, religions and governments have tried to destroy the Bible, persecuting and even killing all who refused to deny its truth; but God's Word has always survived. The Bible has been translated into hundreds of languages and is the most widely distributed book of all times.

❑ Hebrews 4:12 "The word of God is living and powerful."

Q. What does it mean to grow as a Christian?

Just as a baby needs milk to grow, your newly born spirit needs spiritual food:

❑ 1 Peter 2:2 "As newborn babes, desire the pure milk of the word, that you may grow thereby."

- Read and study the Bible:

  God's Word will help you to know Him and to understand His will and purpose for your life.

- Pray daily:

  God desires to be your closest friend. Take time to talk to God and listen to Him every day.

- Attend church regularly:

  Find a Bible-believing church where you can worship God, learn from a pastor and good Bible teachers, make Christian friends, and be part of God's work in your community.

- Be baptized (if you haven't been baptized already):

  God instructs us to be baptized as a sign to God and others that we have decided to follow Jesus Christ.

- Be led by the Holy Spirit:

  As a Christian, God's Spirit lives in you. Be sensitive to what God wants, and allow God to direct you in every area of your life.

- Tell others about Jesus:

  The gospel (or "Good News") of Jesus Christ is for everyone, and God wants us to share this news with others.

Q. What are common challenges for new Christians?

- What if I can't understand the Bible?

  God will help you to understand and apply His Word to your life. God is the One who led each of the Bible writers to write exactly what He wanted to say. Since God lives in you, as a Christian, He will help you understand what He meant. Other Christians, such as a Sunday school teacher or a pastor, can also help you understand and apply God's Word to your life.

- What happens when I am tempted to sin again?

  When a temptation comes, you have a choice—either to resist the temptation or to sin. As a follower of Jesus, it is very important to stay as far away from evil as possible and to draw closer to God. It's important to avoid places or situations that could tempt you to sin or negative people who could pressure you to do wrong things. God will help you to do what is right, and His Holy Spirit—who is now inside you—will convict your heart (or help you to "know" inwardly) when you have done something wrong.

  When we sin, the Bible says:

❑   1 John 1:9   "If we confess our sins, He is faithful and just to forgive us our sins and to cleanse us from all unrighteousness."

- What about my non-Christian friends?

  God wants us to love everyone, and He wants us to show people how wonderful He is through our love, our kindness, and the way we live. We are to be a light for Jesus and a witness to our friends by sharing our faith in Him.

It is a good thing to train a child in biblical knowledge and help him or her learn biblical facts. But it is even more important to strengthen and motivate the heart and spirit of a child. Encourage your child to have a holy fear of God, a desire to always love and obey the Lord, and a commitment to wholehearted worship.

CHAPTER 8

Preparing Your Child to Be a Prayer Champion

A true heart for world missions is not something that can be *taught* (although we will certainly try!); it is a revelation of God's heart that must be *caught* from the Lord Himself, through His Word, and through prayer. When it comes to praying with your child, I encourage you not to spend all your time talking about prayer needs or even teaching about prayer. The most effective way to train your child in effective prayer is simply to pray!

Q. Is it possible for my child to really *want* to pray?

Your child can become a champion for God in prayer. He or she can be trained to hear God's voice and can learn to pray in boldness and in faith.

When God spoke to young Samuel in 1 Samuel 3, it wasn't some sweet children's message; God spoke to Samuel as if he were a man, with a tough word for the high priest of all Israel. As teachers and parents, our goal should not be to teach our children to pray cute little prayers to make *us* look good. We must realize that the prayers of a child—even the prayers of *our* children—could change lives and impact nations! A child's simple trust may even challenge and encourage us to rise to a higher level of faith.

CHILDREN PRAYED FOR HOURS, WEEPING FOR THE LOST

A testimony of prayer to read aloud to children

One time at a large camp for children, I simply prayed for God to give the children more of His heart and compassion for the lost. After a time of worship, I felt led to invite any children with unsaved parents to come forward for prayer, and I was completely shocked as over a hundred children came to the altar.

Children began to pray for their parents, as other children came forward to support them. Then something like a wave of God's love and compassion began to pour over the campers. The children started to cry, earnestly interceding for the salvation of these parents, and then fervently interceded for the lost around the world.

I had expected the prayer time to last for only a few minutes, but God had something else in mind! For over two hours, hundreds of children fell to their knees weeping, hugging each other, and praying—like I had never seen children pray. By the time we were done, wadded-up, mushy tissue paper covered the chapel floor, and the prayers of children had covered the earth. It was one of the most incredible ministry experiences of my life!

Prayer time with children is not always spectacular, but it always makes a difference. As we train our children to grow in prayer, God also wants us, as parents and teachers, to develop our own personal prayer life. This takes work, time, and an establishment of new habits; but it's exciting to know that we can grow with our children as we learn to pray.

I once spoke with an international minister who had ministered in hundreds of Christian churches of many different denominational backgrounds. When I mentioned this book and my desire to devote one chapter to the importance of prayer, this man encouraged me not to assume that most Christian parents and teachers are already praying. In congregation after congregation he had asked people to raise their hands if they spent thirty minutes in prayer each day, and unfortunately usually less than 5 percent of his audiences could honestly answer yes.

Although faithful, quality prayer time is something that I believe most of us desire, I will not presume that you (or your child) have already established this discipline in your lives. But I want to encourage you that yes, you can pray!

Q. But what if my child won't pray for more than a minute?

Praying *longer* is not necessarily *better*. However, without training and encouragement, I have found that most children will usually pray for only about thirty seconds (unless they go through their entire list of "God bless Uncle Mitch, Aunt Marilyn, Grandpa and Grandma" . . . and everyone they've ever met).

One of the best ways to encourage your child to establish a deeper relationship with the Lord is simply to set aside more time in your child's day for spiritual development—including more time for personal Bible reading and more time dedicated to prayer. A helpful idea is to encourage children to establish personal Bible reading and prayer goals and to keep track of their weekly progress.

For a while, you could even have a special reward each week or month when your child has met a goal. This isn't bribing children to pray but rather is a celebration of an important new discipline! A child might begin with a goal of praying for thirty minutes a week (which is five minutes a day, six days a week—not counting Sunday church time). After a few successful weeks, your child can then raise his or her prayer goal to perhaps an hour a week (ten minutes a day)—and so on.

At our home in the country, we have a ten-minute "prayer trail" around our property. Before school, our older children begin their day by praying for one or more "prayer laps." My little ones aren't old enough to go out into the woods, but they have their own little five-minute "prayer walk" around the outside of our house.

I have sometimes encouraged the parents in our church to actually set a kitchen timer for five or ten minutes and to encourage their children to go off by themselves to a quiet corner and keep praying—out loud, as hard as they can, from their heart—until the buzzer goes off.

🌐 TEACHING OPPORTUNITY

Practical Ideas to Increase Your Child's Prayer Time

- Sing worship songs, perhaps with a worship CD or tape

- Sit quietly and simply think about God

- Thank God for as many specific things as you can

- Review the fruit of the Spirit (Galatians 5:22–23) and the armor of God (Ephesians 6:13–18)

- Say (and pray) favorite Bible verses as they come to mind

- Review (and commit to obey) God's Ten Commandments (Exodus 20:1–17)

- Go through the Lord's Prayer (Matthew 6:9–13) as a seven-step prayer guide

Q. What do I do if my child's prayer isn't answered?

You may be afraid to have your child pray about specific concerns because it might make God "look bad" if your child's prayer doesn't get answered. But don't be afraid. Let God take care of His own reputation—and let us pray! Encourage your child to be specific in his or her prayers and to pray according to God's will as revealed in the Bible.

There may be times when things happen that we don't understand. Perhaps your child prays for a dying grandparent to get better, and yet the grandparent dies. Many times we will not know why things didn't work out as we had prayed. We may not understand ourselves, and we may not have any answers for our children.

Even so, we can't ignore this opportunity for spiritual training. These are vital times to train our children in steadfast faith. If things happen that we don't understand, we can still encourage our children that God is good and loving and worthy to be praised—*no matter what*!

You may want to refer to some of the missionary biographies included in this book. For example, when missionary Jim Elliot was killed by the people he was trying to reach, his wife, Elisabeth Elliot, proclaimed: "This is not a tragedy. God has a plan and a purpose in all things." God can even take what the enemy meant for bad and turn it around for good. (You can read how the men who killed Jim Elliot are now believers in Christ and even church elders in that tribe!)

Agree together as a family (or as a class) for specific needs. Many people pray such vague prayers that they would never even know if God answered them. For example, instead of praying "God bless all the missionaries . . ." you could pray "Dear Lord, we ask You to provide all the finances needed for Mr. and Mrs. Smith and their family in Peru so they will be able to buy that sound system they need. Speak to people's hearts to give to their ministry, and help the Smiths and their mission organization to make the best choices with the money they receive."

It's exciting when you agree together for a specific request and then see the Lord answer it! Seeing specific answered prayer encourages our faith and motivates us to keep praying.

And when you pray, pray in faith. Instead of praying for things you don't even believe can happen, begin by praying for specific things you *can* believe for—and then ask God to increase your faith! At the same time, don't discourage your child if he or she has faith for something that you do not. Your child's faithful prayers may surprise you!

Q. How can I teach my child to use God's Word in prayer?

One key that will help you pray in faith and believe for answers is to find (and memorize) key Bible verses that deal with the particular circumstances about which you are praying. For example, if you are praying for your Uncle Al to receive the Lord, it would be good to find a few verses that relate to the situation, such as:

- "The Lord is . . . not willing that any should perish . . ." (2 Peter 3:9).

- "Believe on the Lord Jesus Christ, and you will be saved, you and your household" (Acts 16:31).

With these verses, your faith in God can be strengthened and you can believe what you are praying when you say:

"Heavenly Father, Your word says that You don't want Uncle Al to perish. We know that You love him—even more than we do! Your Son even died for Uncle Al so that he could be saved! We ask You to open his eyes to see the truth of the gospel. Let him see how much he needs You. Send someone to witness to him today! You have saved us, Lord, and we ask that all of our household would be saved too, especially Uncle Al. In the name of Jesus, Amen."

🌐 TEACHING OPPORTUNITY

The Lord's Prayer—As a Child's Seven-Step Prayer Guide

Teach your child to pray effectively by using the Lord's Prayer as an outline.

1. Our Father who art in heaven:

   Thank God that you are His child and that He is your perfect Father!

2. Hallowed be Thy name:

Speak out different names or descriptions of God for every letter of the alphabet. Worship God as you think about how He is awesome! Almighty! Abba, Father! Beautiful! Benevolent! Burden-bearer! Creator! Christ! Comforter!

3. Thy kingdom come, Thy will be done on earth, as it is in heaven:

Pray for God's perfect will to be done in your life—for yourself, your family, your school, your church, your city, your state, your country, and for all the leaders in authority over you. Pray for the world: for missions, the poor, unreached people, specific countries, current news, and your missionaries.

4. Give us this day our daily bread:

Ask God for everything you need and for everything your family needs, including an increased "hunger" for God's Word!

5. And forgive us our trespasses (sins), as we forgive those who trespass (sin) against us:

Spend time being quiet before God. Ask Him to show you if you are doing anything that doesn't please Him, and then ask God to forgive you. Be willing to change. Forgive anyone who has sinned against you or hurt your feelings.

6. And lead us not into temptation, but deliver us from evil:

Ask God to help you stay away from sin and bad things. Pray for God to protect you and to keep you safe in Jesus.

7. For Thine is the kingdom and the power and the glory forever:

End with a time of praise. Commit to live for God and His kingdom for the rest of the day—and for the rest of your life.

Q. Are there tools to help train my child in prayer?

Children don't need expensive prayer books or special journals in order to pray; they only need a desire for God. (And if your child doesn't have that, you can ask God to give him or her that desire!) However, just as you might buy a soccer ball and uniform to encourage physical development or reading books to encourage mental development, you could organize some prayer tools to encourage your child's spiritual development.

 **TEACHING OPPORTUNITY**

Establish a Child's Personal Prayer Spot

You may want to set up a corner of your child's bedroom (or your school or church classroom) as a "prayer spot." This could be a comfortable, welcoming place or perhaps a quiet, hidden place.

The following list of "Quiet Time Accessories" may help you to encourage your child in his or her prayer time.

Quiet Time Accessories:

- Personal Bible (that your child can write in)

- Bible-reading chart

- Prayer-time chart

- Bible promise book

- Prayer journal or prayer diary

- World map on the wall

- Child's book about praying for the world (such as *Window on the World*)

- Posters (such as the fruit of the Spirit, the armor of God, the Ten Commandments, or favorite Bible verses)

- Pictures (of friends, relatives, missionaries, people, etc.)

- Comfortable chair or beanbag

- Little table (or box)

- CD or tape player (with worship music or Bible tapes)

- Timer (to set prayer time goals)

A Highly Recommended Prayer Resource:

Window on the World, by Daphne Spraggett and Jill Johnstone (Angus Hudson, Ltd., 2002 by Authentic Media), is an outstanding prayer resource for Christian parents and teachers and highly recommended for every mission-minded child. Filled with stunning full-color glossy photographs, this A to Z overview of one hundred countries and people groups provides an exciting learning experience with many specific ideas to help your child pray for hundreds of prayer needs from all around the world. As a beautiful yet practical hardcover book, *Window on the World* is an excellent resource and my number one choice to help children pray effectively for international needs. (Please refer to the "Recommended Resources" for other great mission-minded prayer tools.)

Q. How can I encourage my child to write in a prayer journal or prayer diary?

A prayer journal is simply a blank notebook used to write thoughts and prayers to the Lord. It provides a context for being open and honest about what the Lord is doing in your life and to express what you are going through. A child can write specific prayers to the Lord or make a list of things to be thankful for.

Some children will enjoy this, and it will become a part of their prayer life. For others, however, it just won't work—and it doesn't have to. My husband is not a "journal person" at all, yet I admire his prayer life more than anyone's. He loves to simply walk outside and pray for hours every day, letting the Lord direct his prayers. We need to encourage our children to pray in a way that works for them.

A prayer journal does not have to be written in every day. You can encourage your child to use a percentage of regular "writing" time (perhaps once or twice a week) to encourage this discipline. But it is important to remember that these journals are for the writer and the Lord only. Personal prayer entries should not be evaluated for correct spelling, grammar, and writing techniques, or even critiqued for proper thinking. Instead, realize this is an opportunity for a child to write simply for personal enjoyment and spiritual growth.

A prayer diary is a tool for keeping a record of day-to-day time in prayer, similar to a daily planner. If you decide to buy a prayer diary, one of the best available is YWAM's *Personal Prayer Diary and Daily Planner*. Along with maps, pictures, a Bible-reading guide, and a daily guide for praying for the world, this resource also includes a weekly calendar and daily schedule organizer with spaces to write down specific daily requests and praise reports. YWAM also has a special diary/journal designed for young people and children entitled *Walking with God*. Both of these prayer tools are highly recommended.

It is very important to teach your child to be flexible and sensitive to the Holy Spirit as you pray each day. It is good to have a plan but even better to be open to God's plans.

When you become aware of a specific prayer request, your child can . . .

- pray about the need right away.

- save the request for dinner or bedtime prayers or a later quiet time.

- write the need in a prayer journal.

- continue praying about the need as God brings it to mind.

When you become aware of a specific answer to prayer, your child can . . .

- say "Thank you, Lord!"

- spend part of his or her quiet time praising God for His faithfulness.

- write the answer in a prayer journal.

- share the great report with others, including both Christians and non-Christians.

Wonderful Memories of Family Prayer Time

All throughout my childhood, my family gathered together before bedtime for a time of family prayers. My parents were amazingly consistent; it didn't matter if we had company with us or even if we were staying somewhere else with friends or relatives. Every evening—the only exception being if we didn't get home until late because of going to a church service—our family came together to pray. Just as some parents yell, "Come and eat!" our family was known throughout the neighborhood for our typical evening call: "Hey kids! It's prayer time!"

This family devotion time was never complicated. My mom usually led us in singing a simple song or two, my dad would read aloud a chapter or two in the Bible, we would go around the room and each of us would thank God for something or pray for specific needs, and then we ended by quoting the Lord's Prayer together. It was our regular evening practice, and it's a heritage of prayer that I've always been thankful for!

TEACHING OPPORTUNITY

Ten Prayer Projects for Your Child

1. Have your child start a prayer journal or prayer diary. For three days, encourage your child to begin writing notes and comments to God for about fifteen minutes a day.

2. Put up a world map in a prominent place and use this as a reminder to encourage your child to pray for other countries and people.

3. Have your child make a photo prayer-collage on a bulletin board, poster board, or in a mini-album. (This doesn't have to be hard. My eight-year-old son, Mark, simply uses push pins to tack photos of various prayer needs around his bed. These pictures remind him, as he drifts off to sleep, to pray for African orphan children, specific missionary friends, and special relatives.)

4. Page through a current newspaper with your child. Find an international need, locate the place on a world map, and then pray together.

5. Make a poster using the Lord's Prayer as a seven-step prayer guide. Draw a large staircase and write each area of prayer on a separate level; then pray through the Lord's Prayer with your child.

6. On the left side of a bulletin board write *Prayer Needs*, and on the right side write *Praise Reports!* Have a stack of 3 x 5 cards for your child to begin writing down specific requests. Pin the cards to the *Prayer Needs* side until they are answered; then have your child write *Answered!* in big red letters across the

card, move it to the *Praise Reports!* side of the bulletin board, and thank God together for His faithfulness.

7. Have your child cut up old magazines to make a poster entitled "Blessed to Be a Blessing!" On one side glue magazine pictures of things to be thankful for (food, clothes, appliances, toys, homes, etc.). On the other side glue pictures of international people in need (gathered from world relief magazines or magazines like *National Geographic* or printed off of mission-oriented websites). Use the poster to encourage your child to thank God for His blessings and to seek Him for how to use these blessings to help others.

8. Make a copy of a one-page world map and then cut it into continental sections. Fold the pieces and place them in a bowl. Have your child select one of the pieces of paper each day and pray for that particular continent. In seven days your child will pray for every continent!

9. Get a stack of *National Geographic* or missionary magazines and have your child cut out faces of people from all over the world. Put these in a box. Have your child pull out a picture and use it as a starting point for prayer—not necessarily for the particular person in the photo, but for general world needs that come to mind (such as the needs of African orphans, or poor mothers in India, or people who worship idols and need to hear the gospel).

10. Organize a special "Prayer Spot" for your child (in a closet, a corner of a room, or some other special place). Put up a world map and photos of people groups to pray for; and have some prayer tools nearby, such as a Bible, missions books, and a prayer journal.

🌐 TEACHING OPPORTUNITY

Prayer Ideas for Your Location and Leaders

As you train your child to pray for other nations of the world, encourage your child to also pray for your own country and your own leaders. As you learn your country's history, learn about the spiritual history (what God has done) in your nation. Find the names of your national and local leaders who are in positions of authority (including teachers, coaches, music instructors, pastors, and children's ministers), and encourage your child to remember to pray for these people.

Our children have also participated in and helped to organize several local open-air meetings (at critical times of need) to pray for local, national, and international leaders—along with publicly proclaiming God's Good News. A mission-minded child is always on the lookout for creative ways to share the gospel!

CHAPTER 9

Missions and Money

"For where your treasure is, there your heart will be also."
—Jesus Christ (Matthew 6:21)

In our family's ministry office, a carved wooden bowl displays simple coins from all around the world. Most of the pieces are dull and worn, while some are new and shiny. Our children often enjoy fingering the various francs from France, pulas from Botswana, and euros from Europe, to mention just a few. My favorite is an intricate gold-and-silver-colored piece from Italy, although, as with most of these coins, I have no idea of its worth. Some of the coins are no longer in circulation; some of the countries they're from no longer exist. All are simply extra pocket change left over from years of past mission trips, each saved as little souvenirs and little reminders that money is only a temporary "little thing." Each coin is (or was) valuable only because some government somewhere determined it would have value.

But money is also a "big thing"—and we can't underestimate the importance of training our children to have a godly perspective toward money and financial stewardship. Our money represents our life: our time, our talents, our education and experiences, and our priorities. In fact, if we really want to find out what is important to us, we can simply look back through our checkbooks and credit card statements over the past few months. Our true priorities are right there in black and white (or red!); and the numbers don't lie.

It's really very simple. If we have a heart for the Lord and for the lost, we will give our resources to glorify Him and to help spread His gospel; and if our children are raised with this perspective, it will affect their bottom-line attitude toward the purpose of money. As mission-minded Christians, we need to come to the realization that our resources are not really "ours" anyway. Both parents and children need to acknowledge regularly that *everything* we have ultimately belongs to God: our life is God's, our home (or bedroom) is God's, our car (or bicycle, or special toy) is God's, our money is God's. We're all simply stewards of God's "stuff."

"I'm not called to go; I'm called to give."

You may have heard this common statement in regard to missions: "Some are called to go, but others are called to pray or to give." I believe this is true—and that *all* of us as Christians are *equally* called to do our unique part in helping to fulfill the Great Commission. Whether we're called to go or to pray or to give, the level of commitment to God's purposes should be the same for all of us; and this is a vital principle to instill in the next generation.

As we train our children, we need to emphasize that God has blessed each of us for a bigger purpose than merely to satisfy our own wants and desires. Like Abraham, God has blessed us to establish His covenant on the earth. If *your* part (or your child's part) in helping to fulfill His Great Commission is to support world missions financially, then you need to trust God to meet your needs, and you need to begin to expand your desire to help others.

If you or your child is called to be a "giver," then begin to think (and dream) about what your money and future financial resources could do for God. Instead of browsing through department stores, catalogs, and eBay, be on the lookout for projects and people that God may want you to support. Of course, we must provide for our personal needs and prepare for our future, but as stewards of God's Great Commission we must be willing to abandon our dreams for God's dream!

One Child and a Few Coins Make a Big Difference

One young boy named Ethan heard of a mission project to sponsor a little Ugandan orphan boy at our ministry's new orphanage. Although he was only eight years old, Ethan wanted to sponsor this child personally; and with his mother's permission, he made the commitment. Right away Ethan began collecting coins from all around his house. He started asking his friends at church if they could donate spare change to help an orphan. And he set up a simple lemonade and cookie stand in a parking lot near his house. With homemade signs covered with marking-pen exclamation points and a photo of his new African friend, Ethan soon raised over six months of full orphan support—all on his own initiative.

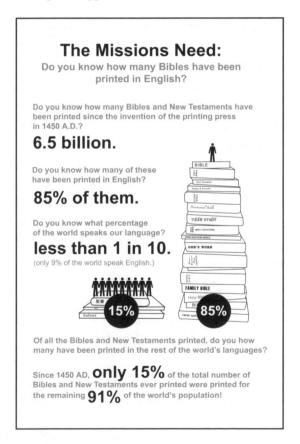

As he presented his first donation, this young boy was so excited to make a big difference in the life of an African orphan. His family and friends were inspired by his generosity, and many other people (including both adults and children) were so challenged by his testimony that they wanted to step out in a greater way to do something for others.

— 👫 FROM MY CHILDREN'S PERSPECTIVE —

"KIDS CAN RAISE MONEY FOR MISSIONS!"
By Daniel Dunagan, age eleven

Even kids can raise money for missions, especially if we join together with a specific goal! Over the years, I've seen plenty of ways that kids can earn money for missions, and it can be fun.

Sometimes our children's church has put up a "thermometer" poster with a certain missions goal, and when we've gotten to the top, we've celebrated with an ice cream or pizza party. Once our class bought a stove for an overseas family, and another time we bought puppets for missionaries in Japan. For me, it seems to help when there's a picture of what we're working toward, because then I can "see" where my money is going. We raised money to buy stuffed animals for an orphanage, we bought gospel booklets for missionary kids to distribute, and two times our children's class bought bikes to help national ministers in India.

One time when I was at church, I heard about some kids in Africa who were really poor. One story in particular really touched me. I heard about this little kid who had only an old sweatshirt—no shorts, not even any underwear—and the kid was about my age! I heard that anytime a person would come around him, this kid would pull his old sweatshirt down because he was so embarrassed.

The whole next week, I was constantly thinking about this kid. I thought about how horrible it would be to be so poor. I just couldn't get it out of my head.

The Missions Need:
Do you know how the Christian Church
spends every dollar?

96.8 cents
of each dollar
is spent on the 2 billion people
who call themselves Christians.
(Christians spending money on themselves)

2.9 cents
of each dollar
is spent in those who have
heard and rejected Christ.

only .3 cents
of each dollar
(only one-third of a penny) **is spent to**
reach the 1.6 billion people throughout the
world who have NEVER heard or had a
chance to respond to Jesus Christ.

Then one night, I thought about it so much, I started crying. I realized that a couple U.S. dollars could buy me some candy or a toy, but for the same amount of money, I could buy a new outfit for that one poor kid.

That night in my room, I decided to do as much as I could. I had some money that I had been saving to open a bank account and to get some things I wanted. But right then, I determined to help as many kids as possible. Only my mom knew about it at the time, but she asked me to share about it so maybe others would be encouraged to give. I do know that the next Sunday, when I slipped my entire savings into the missions offering, all I could think about was how good I felt inside. Altogether our kids' class clothed an entire African village, and I knew that I had had a part!

 TEACHING OPPORTUNITY

Mission-Minded Memory, Oratorical Practice, or Reading Aloud ("My Choice" Poem)

Note: Before reading this simple poem, discuss with your child the blessings of your lives and how we need to surrender all of our blessings to God. This poem was written by a young man named Bill McChesney as he thought about his "rights" and "choices" and then surrendered everything to the Lord. Afterward, he went to Africa and served the Lord for several years as a missionary in the Congo. During a military uprising in that country in 1964, Bill McChesney was tragically killed at the age of only twenty-eight. But this young man had already "given his life" long before that particular day; his choice for all eternity was total obedience to the Lord Jesus Christ.

 MY CHOICE

By Bill McChesney

I want my breakfast served at "Eight,"
With ham and eggs upon the plate;
A well-broiled steak I'll eat at "One,"
And dine again when day is done.

I want an ultramodern home,
And in each room a telephone;
Soft carpets, too, upon the floors,
And pretty drapes to grace the doors.

A cozy place of lovely things
Like easy chairs with innersprings.
And then I'll get a small TV—
Of course, "I'm careful what I see."

I want my wardrobe, too, to be,
Of neatest, finest quality,
With latest style in suit and vest,
Why shouldn't Christians have the best?

But then the Master I can hear,
In no uncertain voice, so clear,
"I bid you come and follow Me,
The Lowly Man of Galilee.

Birds of the air have made their nest,
And foxes in their holes find rest;
But I can offer you no bed;
No place have I to lay my head."

In shame I hung my head and cried,
How could I spurn the Crucified?
Could I forget the way He went,
The sleepless nights in prayer He spent?

For forty days without a bite,
Alone He fasted day and night;
Despised, rejected—on He went,
And did not stop 'till veil He rent.

A Man of sorrows and of grief—
"Smitten of God," the prophet said—
Mocked, beaten, bruised,
His blood ran red.

If He be God and died for me,
No sacrifice too great can be
For me, a mortal man, to make;
I'll do it all for Jesus' sake.

Yes, I will tread the path He trod,
No other way will please my God;
So henceforth this my choice shall be,
My choice for all eternity.

∅ TEACHING OPPORTUNITY

Fifteen Ideas to Raise Money for Missions

1. Have your child decorate a special container, perhaps with a photo, and begin saving coins for a specific mission project.

2. For special missions offerings in children's church or a Sunday school class, use attention-grabbing collection plates such as empty coconut shells or African-looking baskets.

3. If raising money for a building project, make a poster of a brick wall and have your child color in bricks (or attach paper bricks) as you advance toward your goal.

4. If raising money for Bibles, make a poster of a stack of Bibles and have your child color in Bibles (or attach paper Bibles) as you advance toward your goal. Decorate with stacks of Bibles.

5. Make a "thermometer" to chart a specific missions goal.

6. Share a fun mission-minded fundraising idea with a leader from your church. One idea is to have a coin-collecting race between your church's youth group and children's department. Both groups could use the same designated coin, or the youth could collect one type of coin (for example, nickels) and the children could collect another type of coin (for example, dimes)—with the idea of seeing which department can raise more money.

7. Help your child collect aluminum cans for recycling, or encourage other families (or children in your church) to canvas their neighborhood and collect cans for a specific mission project.

8. Have your child collect coins and tape them to a long streamer. This idea could also be used in a class, with two groups (perhaps boys vs. girls) competing to see who can reach a predetermined streamer distance first.

9. Your child could find a specific mission project to support, collecting coins from other families as he or she shares this need.

10. Have a family yard sale with all proceeds going for missions, and have your child help with the details.

11. Work with your child to organize a children's bazaar, with handmade arts and crafts, or baked goods, and give all the proceeds to missions.

12. Work with your child to plan a neighborhood missions carnival, with fun booths, popcorn, pop, and candy—with all proceeds going to missions.

13. Your child could offer to do work for family or friends (such as housecleaning, laundry, or yard work) in exchange for people donating toward a specific mission project. A variation of this idea is to have a church "slave auction," where children or youth are auctioned to the highest bidder for a set amount of hours of work, and the proceeds are given to missions.

14. Your family could host a special missions banquet for adults or a formal event for teens and young adults, and donate all the proceeds to missions.

15. Have a "multiply your talents" project. Give your child a certain amount of money with the mission-minded purpose of using this money, along with his or her talents, abilities, and creativity, for a specified length of time (perhaps two weeks or one month) to raise money for a specific mission project. Your child could use the money to buy gas for a lawn mower, to buy lemonade to sell on the corner, or to buy ingredients for a neighborhood bake sale. At the end of the designated time have your child return the original money, along with the surplus he or she raised, and give it toward the mission project.

CHAPTER **10**

World Missions and Your Local Church

"The mission of the church is missions."
—David Livingstone

Is "world missions" *your* church's mission? This was Livingstone's proclamation; yet in far too many of today's congregations, it's too far from true. Take a moment to consider with your child the emphasis on local and foreign missions in your home church:

- How often is God's love for the world emphasized?

- What are the names of the different missionaries your church supports, where do they live, and what is each missionary's particular ministry focus?

- Is your congregation regularly encouraged and challenged to share the gospel?

- Does your church's Sunday school or children's church program emphasize the needs of the world?

Regardless of your current situation, perhaps God has placed you and your child as His mission-minded ambassadors in your local church. Just as Esther stepped forward to help save her people in the foreign land of Persia, you may be called to impact your congregation "for such a time as this." As you encourage your local church to support missions more effectively, you could have a vital role in the gospel reaching many unsaved people.

Q. How can we encourage missions in our local church?

Here are ten practical ideas for you and your child to promote an increased heart for the nations in your local church: help create a mission-minded atmosphere; start a prayer group; support your missionaries; encourage your pastor to go on a missions trip; promote world missions in every department; help your children's department to focus on world needs; purchase mission books; encourage your church to sponsor an adoption project; participate in a church-sponsored missionary outreach.

• Idea #1—Help create a mission-minded atmosphere

When newcomers enter your church building (or your church children's department), can they visually "see" a heart-emphasis toward missions? In some church sanctuaries, international flags reflect a worldwide vision. In some church lobbies, missionary maps and newsletters encourage people to pray. In some church lobbies, maps showing where missionaries are located and newsletters from those missionaries encourage people to pray. In some church hallways, missions souvenirs fill display cases and hint of awaiting adventure.

Years ago I was impacted by my first visit to a wonderful mission-minded church. A giant world map covered the entire lobby wall, a row of clocks displayed current time zones from around the world, and below each clock hung an exciting missionary picture. The preaching (and written literature) was also focused on world missions, but it was the large wall display that left the long-term impression. The mission of that church was obvious, and the atmosphere reinforced it.

🌐 TEACHING OPPORTUNITY

Mission-Minded Church Decorating Ideas

You and your child could help decorate a wall at your church, a Sunday school bulletin board, or a special table with a mission-minded focus. You could also present a particular mission-atmosphere idea to your pastor or children's administrator. One idea would be to ask if your church or children's department would be interested in displaying international flags (either small or large) to represent each country where your church's missionaries serve. You and your child could help to raise the funds for this project.

- **Idea #2—Start a mission-minded prayer group (for children or families)**

Does your church pray for the world? Some churches set aside regular prayer services for world missions (perhaps weekly or monthly). Other congregations have daily corporate prayer times to intercede for both the needs of the local church and foreign missionaries.

Even a small weekly or monthly home prayer meeting (or a church cell group) with a mission-minded emphasis can make a tremendous impact on your church, your missionaries, and the world. And it doesn't have to be difficult!

⬤ TEACHING OPPORTUNITY

Fifteen Steps to a Great Mission-Minded Prayer Meeting

1. Invite people.

2. Make sure your house, or meeting location, is clean.

3. As people arrive, greet them with a smile.

4. Offer something to drink, such as water, juice, coffee, or tea.

5. Gather together and open your meeting with a prayer.

6. Worship God by singing a few songs or reading a psalm.

7. Take turns reading and discussing a few Bible verses about missions and reaching the lost. (See chapter 4 for specific ideas.)

8. Read an encouraging missions motto or short missions quote.

9. Highlight a famous missions hero and/or one current missionary.

10. Present an international news update. Use *Window on the World*, *Operation World*, highlights from the World Prayer Team (www.worldprayerteam.org), recent missionary newsletters, or current international news from a newspaper or an online news source. You could perhaps have the group watch a brief online video news segment on a laptop computer as a focal point for prayer.

11. Spend most of your time praying specifically (and fervently) for international needs and missionary prayer requests.

12. Share any announcements (perhaps about a current mission project).

13. Stand in a circle and close with prayer.

14. End with a time of fellowship, perhaps with a simple international snack.

15. Thank everyone for coming, and say goodbye at the door.

Note: To help facilitate this meeting, assign specific responsibilities to different people—a greeter, a worship leader, a person to share a missions motto and a missionary highlight, a person to read the Bible verses, someone to share an international news update, several prayer leaders, someone to announce upcoming mission projects, and someone to prepare the snacks.

TEACHING OPPORTUNITY

Fifteen Projects for Your Mission-Minded Prayer Group

1. Have a fundraiser for a specific mission project.

2. Have a car wash for one of your missionaries.

3. Have a multi-family garage sale for missions.

4. Gather items for a missionary care package.

5. Put together a special gift for MKs (missionary kids).

6. Put together gift packets for an orphanage.

7. "Adopt" a child or an unreached people group.

8. Sign a card to give to one of your missionaries.

9. Make a welcome basket for a visiting missionary.

10. Have a birthday party for missionary kids (at any time!).

11. Have a missionary share with your group.

12. Hold an international potluck or try a particular foreign food.

13. Share about Jesus with someone in your neighborhood.

14. Do something nice for a foreign exchange student.

15. Reach out to a local international family.

- ## Idea #3—Encourage your church's missionaries

You would be amazed at what a big difference a little bit of encouragement can make. Missionaries need much more than financial support; they need prayer, they need encouragement, and (like all of us!) they need friends. There are unlimited ways that you and your child can encourage your church's missionaries. Here are a few ideas to get you started.

🌐 TEACHING OPPORTUNITY

Fifteen Ways to Encourage Your Church's Missionaries

1. Learn the names of your missionaries and their children.
2. Read the newsletters they send to your church.
3. If they have an e-mail newsletter, sign up to receive them.
4. Pray specifically for their needs.
5. Send an encouraging e-mail to their family.
6. Write an old-fashioned letter or send a fun card.
7. Put together a personal gift package for their family—for Christmas, or for no particular reason.
8. Share their news with other people in your church.
9. Put their family photo on your refrigerator.
10. Greet them and invite them to lunch when they visit.
11. Stay tuned to international news that affects them.
12. Send a quick e-mail just to say "Hi!"
13. Pray specifically for their children.
14. Have your child send encouraging e-mails to a missionary kid.
15. Be their friend.

• Idea #4—Encourage your senior pastor to take a mission trip

Mission-minded pastors will typically schedule regular short-term mission outreaches for themselves and others in the congregation. Even a one to two week trip (possibly only missing one Sunday) to a foreign location can help realign your church's mission priority, refresh your pastor's local and international vision, and renew your pastor's perspective for ministry among the people in your congregation.

At one time our senior pastor needed a time of rest and decided to take a ten-month mission trip/sabbatical to the Philippines. During that season, my husband (a missionary evangelist) served as our church's interim pastor while continuing to lead several short-term mission outreaches. Despite our pastor's absence, or perhaps *because* of our pastor's strong missions emphasis, the congregation did not suffer, but continued to grow.

• Idea #5—Encourage a vision for missions in every department

In a truly mission-minded church, "world missions" is not a separate department but a foundation in every area. You and your child can encourage this focus. Whenever a short-term mission team comes or goes, be available for encouragement, prayer, or financial support. If anyone from your church feels called to mission work, show interest as this person seeks God's will and invest time to nurture what God is doing in his or her heart.

As you are involved in a particular ministry (men's, women's, youth, children, Bible studies, home groups, etc.), allow your missions perspective to "flavor" that ministry. A Bible study could include a discussion about how to more actively fulfill God's Great Commission; a membership class could include information about your church's missions focus; free time at a church retreat could be used to share about an international passion.

If you meet a high school or college student searching for life purpose, present a few adventurous ideas or give a challenge to research a specific mission organization. With a little encouragement, youth can instill an infectious zeal for missions into a congregation. Youth can lead missions fundraisers, have their own prayer services for the nations, or go on short-term outreaches with a church-sponsored group or with organizations such as YWAM, Teen Missions, or Teen Mania.

 TEACHING OPPORTUNITY

Mission-Minded Scholarship Contest

Organize or sponsor an annual "mission-minded scholarship contest" for your church's high school and college-age students. Have students participate by presenting a short speech on a particular missions topic, designing a missions recruiting poster, or performing a special music and/or dramatic presentation. Require an application, several recommendations, and a personal interview to evaluate necessary spiritual maturity. The prize is an all-expense-paid mission trip to visit one of your church's missionaries (to give the church a current report) or to join an outreach with an approved youth organization. This would be something that your child could look forward to as he or she gets older.

- **Idea #6—Encourage a mission-minded children's ministry**

World missions can be a major theme in your children's church and/or Sunday school program. Children can support their own missionaries and raise money for their own significant mission projects. (Our church just finished a children's project to clothe one hundred African children in a remote Ugandan village.) You could decorate your classroom walls with maps and missions photos and make an "international post-office box" to collect letters for your church's missionaries.

Children can enjoy listening to stories of famous missionaries from the past and exciting stories about missionaries today. Along with challenges to accept Christ, there can also be prayer times, as the Lord leads, for children to dedicate their lives totally to God's perfect will—whatever that may be. As some of your church families begin to travel overseas (which is quite common among mission-minded churches), encourage children from your congregation to give testimonies from firsthand mission experiences.

- **Idea #7—Purchase missions books for your church**

Does your church library (and/or bookstore) include a great collection of mission-minded books? If not, perhaps you could obtain permission to start adding a few new missions books each month.

Include famous missionary biographies, teaching books, practical missionary resources, and motivational missions stories for each major age group. This simple idea could encourage and influence many people in your congregation, both now and for years to come.

- ### Idea #8—As your church raises missions funds, raise missions passion

Most churches have specific times for raising money for missions. As these opportunities arise, use your enthusiasm to talk positively about the opportunity. Even more vital than raising missions funds is raising missions enthusiasm and instilling excitement about expanding God's kingdom.

One of the best ways I have seen for a church to instill a passion for missions is to regularly send lay people from the congregation overseas. In our home church, half of our regular missions commitment supports full-time missionaries and the other half goes into a fund to send members of our own congregation on mission trips.

Before a trip, team members will want to share their vision for missions and their heart for the people who don't yet know Jesus. During the outreach, the congregation will naturally want to pray for them. And following the outreach, these new church-member-missionaries (while still "contagious" with a missionary fever!) will want to share their exciting reports. As a result, others will get inspired about missions, will want to support world missions, and will be encouraged to go on the next mission outreach.

- ### Idea #9—Encourage your church to sponsor an "adoption"

Your church could *adopt an unreached people group* as their own. The congregation could take personal responsibility to learn about this particular people group, pray specifically for them, raise money for projects and missionary translation work geared toward them, and organize short-term mission trips to learn about their needs. Perhaps someone from your congregation will be called to become a long-term missionary to these people.

A local church could *adopt a "sister city" or a "sister church"* across the world. Just after the collapse of the former Soviet Union, a large church I knew of spent an entire year evangelizing the city of St. Petersburg, Russia. This local congregation took personal responsibility to reach the people in "their" sister city. They worked to establish a new sister church in that city, and for an entire year the church sent short-term outreach teams every month.

Perhaps your church could *adopt an overseas children's orphanage.* Families could be encouraged to "adopt" a specific orphan or an orphanage house through prayer and designated support. Your church could have specific projects to send supplies or to build an orphanage building, and ongoing support could help feed and clothe the children and allow them to hear the gospel.

— 👫 FROM MY CHILDREN'S PERSPECTIVE —

"WE'VE GOT FRIENDS AROUND THE WORLD!"

By Mark Dunagan, age ten;
Caela Rose Dunagan, age eight; and Philip Dunagan, age five

It's exciting to have friends from around the world! Kids in our family and many friends from our local children's church are now "kid's-prayer-partners" with boys and girls from our ministry's orphanage in Africa. We pray for each other, we have our friends' pictures hanging by our beds, and we even send special gifts and letters back and forth. Having a heart for missions is great—it's simply having fun with new friends from around the world, and helping other people . . . who are a lot like us!

• Idea #10—Participate in a short-term outreach from your church

Perhaps you (or another member of your congregation) could recruit a team of youth, children, adults, or families to go on a group mission outreach. This team could visit and assist one of your church's missionaries or join together with an established mission organization. Lives (both within your congregation and overseas) will likely be changed forever as individuals see the need for missions firsthand.

Sometimes it is falsely assumed that directing extra missions funds to "inexperienced lay people" will only deplete the church's regular missionary support. In actuality, the opposite usually takes place. God's missions funds are not limited. As new short-term missionaries launch out— with their friends and family members supporting missions and praying for missions like never before—a church's heart for missions will multiply.

🌐 TEACHING OPPORTUNITY

Explore Mission Trip Possibilities

Research mission opportunities with your child. Look up different opportunities for short-term mission outreaches that allow children to participate. (See page 224.)

— 👫 FROM MY CHILDREN'S PERSPECTIVE —

"A HEART FOR HELPING ORPHANS"

By Christi Dunagan, age fifteen

Eight-year-old Jennifer huddled in the dark corner of her grandmother's hut. Once again, she was locked in this repulsive room with no food and no hope. Sometimes she was left alone for days while her grandmother wasted what little money they had. Most likely, the old woman would return home—drunk—and beat the girl until she could barely stand.

Jennifer knew nothing of happiness. When she was very young, her parents were victims of Uganda's number one killer: AIDS; and now, she was yet another victim: of poverty, hunger, and abuse.

Hearing footsteps outside her door, Jennifer looked up hopefully. Maybe she would finally be released from this small damp prison she was forced to call home . . . but no. She cringed as the footsteps drew nearer and she recognized them, not as those of her grandmother but as the sound of one of her uncles. Again one was coming. Too often they came to use little Jennifer to satisfy their physical pleasures. When they had enough of her, they left her once again hurt and crying on the mud floor. The latch creaked and Jennifer prepared herself for yet another night of agony and heartache.

She knew she could not last much longer. . . .

* * *

Somehow, the frightened girl escaped and began wandering her village streets. With nowhere to go, Jennifer leaned against the closest building she could find . . . and wept.

A hand touched her shoulder, startling her; but as she looked up, the girl stared into the face of a kind woman. It was Alice, a longtime friend of my family and the local director of an AIDS orphanage that my parents helped establish ten years ago in Mbarara, Uganda.

Along with hundreds of other orphans, this child finally has a home. People are now feeding her, ministering to her hurts, and loving her. Slowly she is learning life is not just pain and horror, and she is discovering joy. Slowly her emotional wounds are healing. Finally Jennifer is becoming the girl she was born to be.

* * *

Recently I had the incredible experience of traveling to Uganda along with my mother and a precious elderly minister. There I met Jennifer and many orphans just like her—and it made an incredible impact on my life. Beginning on that trip, my mom and I have been establishing a brand-new orphanage (called "Oh Sunny Day Village") primarily for AIDS victims. There are many details—organizing orphan photos, recruiting sponsors, doing computer work—but it's worth it. I want to help rescue as many hurting children as I can.

During my journey, I traveled by a rugged dugout canoe to a remote island. There the poverty was so great, and many children were left as orphans due to the trauma of war and AIDS. My mom and I decided we couldn't just sit back. Thousands of children were dying from malnutrition and neglect. We knew we had to do something.

As I walked through the narrow village streets, the air reeked of fish, body odor, and garbage. Little children flocked around me, holding my hands, touching my hair, and gazing deeply into my eyes. As they longed for some sort of love and affection, I wished I could just "wrap them up," hide them in my suitcase, and take them all home.

But obviously that wasn't possible.

Yet since our return home, my mom and I have been working with some Ugandan nationals to build an orphanage on that island for as many children as possible. Our desire is for these orphan children to grow up in an environment where they will be loved and wanted, to provide a happy place where hurting children can receive quality care, nutrition, and education.

Right now our new orphanage is small, but we have a big vision. We started with thirty orphans in a few existing huts and quickly expanded to seventy-five orphans (whom we've just found sponsors for) in eight new orphanage houses; but our goal is to reach many more children. My mom and I know we will never be able to help every orphan in Uganda, but we're doing what we can, and we won't give up.

For these seventy-five children, it is finally an "Oh Sunny Day." No longer will they roam the streets, beg for meals, or sleep "wherever." These little ones will be safe and cared for.

And with smiles on their faces—just like Jennifer now has—these orphans will finally have a chance to become the children they were born to be.

(Note: The official African name for our new orphanage is Osanidde Village. In less than a year, this orphanage has grown to reach 160 children full-time in sixteen new orphanage houses. *Osanidde* is a word in many Luganda worship songs that children love to sing; it sounds just like "Oh Sunny Day!" and means "You are worthy!")

CHAPTER **11**

Making Missions Fun— At Home, School, and Church

Sometimes changing those "big things" in our lives—altering our core attitudes and priorities for education and abandoning our rights—can start with a few "little things" in practical areas of our lives. If we want to begin making a change—to give a greater priority to the Lord and His heart for the world—it can help to keep these goals before us: on our walls, on our calendars, and on our lips (what we say and even what we eat!).

Decorate with a Heart for Missions!

Giving your home (or classroom) a missions focus can begin by simply displaying a world map in a prominent place, putting an atlas or an inspiring missions book on your coffee table, or decorating a mission-minded bulletin board.

In our home, we want our family's passion for world missions to be unmistakable to everyone who visits us. An entire wall of our family room is covered by a huge world map (it's actually wallpaper), and our ministry office/guest room is decorated completely African-style: with leopard-style carpet and bedding, our own souvenirs from Uganda, Rwanda, and Congo, and many exciting missionary photos. The emphasis is constantly before our children (and us); and when guests come to visit, these focal points are often conversation starters to help inspire others to increase their heart for world missions.

It's a scriptural principle: If we want God's Word to be established in our children's hearts, we should constantly keep it in front of our children's eyes and ears. As God inspired Moses to exhort His people Israel, "These words which I command you today shall be in your heart. You shall teach them diligently to your children, and shall talk of them when you sit in your house, when you walk by the way, when you lie down, and when you rise up. . . . You shall write them on the doorposts of your house and on your gates" (Deuteronomy 6:6–9).

Sing International Songs

Music is powerful! It can be used to express our praise as we glorify God, or it can be used for evil. Music can tell us so much about a culture. Songs can help us learn a foreign language, and just listening to the variety of styles can give us a "feel" for another land.

Reflecting on my various missionary experiences, I realize how the music of the people is an integral part of my memories. Africa would not be the same without tribal drums and village rhythms, and a visit to Austria is not complete without a taste of classical Mozart. Think about Jewish folk dancing, Jamaican calypso, and Asian clanging and minor chording; music is an essential and often inseparable part of culture.

As you expose your child to music, include music appreciation (including Western classical music and a variety of international music) as well as the practical study of music (including instrumental and voice instruction). Each area is important to the study of music and all can be of benefit to a mission-minded child. Music can be an important tool to help share the Good News; music can be utilized to attract people to a meeting; the message or anointing in music can soften a person's heart to respond to the gospel; and through heartfelt worship, music can draw us closer to the Lord.

🌐 TEACHING OPPORTUNITY

Mission-Minded Music Ideas

The following songs can be used to encourage your child to have a heart for international missions. It can be fun to attempt to sing in a foreign language or to learn a new mission-minded verse to add to a familiar chorus.

- **Jesus Loves Me**

  (English)
  Jesus loves me, this I know
  For the Bible tells me so,
  Little ones to him belong,
  They are weak, but He is strong.
  Chorus:
  Yes, Jesus loves me (3x)
  The Bible tells me so.

  (Missions verse)
  Jesus loves the na-a-tions
  Every tongue and every tribe,
  And He wants to u-use you
  To reach them to be his bride.
  Yes, Jesus loves them (3x)
  The Bible tells me so.

  (Spanish)
  Chorus: Cristo me ama (3x)
  La Biblia dice asi.

(Spanish pronunciation)
Cree-sto may-aa-ma (3x)
La Bee-Blia dee-say aa-see.

(Swahili pronunciations)
Chorus:
Yay-soo ah-nee pen-da (3x)
Bee-blee-ah ah-nee say mah.

(French pronunciations)
Chorus:
Wee, Zhay-zuee meh-mer (3x)
La Bee-bler dee teh-se.

(Arabic pronunciations)
Chorus:
Kahd faa-kah hub-nah (3x)
Ye-hib-bu-nah Yah-so.

(Russian pronunciations)
Chorus:
Lyoo-beet Ee-ee-soos (3x)
E-to tvyer-do snah-yoo yah.

(Japanese pronunciations)
Chorus:
Wah-gah Shoo Yah-soo (3x)
Way-ray oh ah-ee-soo.

• **God Is So Good**

(English)
God is so good (3x)
He's so good to me.

(Spanish)
Dios bueno es (3x)
Bueno es mi Dios.

(Spanish pronunciation)
Dee-oas boo-way-no-ace (3x)
Boo-way-no-ace me Dee-oas.

(Kitumba—Democratic Republic of Congo)
Nzambi ke mbote (3x)
Ke mbotye na mono.

(Kitumba pronunciation)
Na-zam-bee kay mm-bo-tay (3x)
Kay mm-bo-tay nah mo-no.

- **Praise Him**

    (English)
    Praise Him, Praise Him,
    Praise Him in the morning
    Praise Him in the noontime.
    Praise Him, Praise Him,
    Praise Him when the sun goes down.

    (Luganda—Uganda)
    Tumutende, Tumutende,
    Tumutende nga bukende
    Tumutende nga mutuntu.
    Tumutende, Tumutende,
    Tumutende nga buwungela.

(Luganda pronunciation)
Too-moo-ten-day, Too-moo-ten-day,
Too-moo-ten-day n-Gah boo-kan-day
Too-moo-ten-day n-Gah moo-toon-too.
Too-moo-ten-day, Too-moo-ten-day,
Too-moo-ten-day n-Gah boo-woon-gay-lah.

• This Is the Day

(English)
This is the day (2x)
That the Lord has made (2x)
I will rejoice (2x)
And be glad in it (2x)
This is the day that the Lord has made,
I will rejoice and be glad in it.
This is the day (2x)
That the Lord has made.

(Indonesian)
Hari ini (2x)
Hari ya Tuhan (2x)
Mari kita (2x)
Pujilah Tuhan (2x)
Hari ini hari ya Tuhan,
Mari kita pujulah Tuhan.
Hari ini (2x)
Hari ya Tuhan.

(Indonesian pronunciation)
He-ree eenie (2x)
He-ree ya too-haan (2x)
Maa-ree kee-ta (2x)
Poo-jee-laa too-haan (2x)

He-ree eenie he-ree ya too-haan,
Maa-ree kee-ta poo-jee-laa too-haan.
He-ree eenie (2x)
He-ree ya too-haan.

• The B-I-B-L-E

The B-I-B-L-E
Yes, that's the book for me!
I stand alone on the Word of God
The B-I-B-L-E.

(Missions verse)
The B-I-B-L-E
It has one story, you see,
To tell all nations of God's love
The B-I-B-L-E.

• How Great Thou Art

(English)
Then sings my soul,
My Savior, God, to thee
How great thou art,
How great thou art (all 2x).

(Hungarian pronunciations)
See-vehm feh-lahd,
Ooy-yohng er-rerm-tah-lay
Meely nady vady Tay,
Meely nady vady Tay (all 2x).

(Missions verse)
Oh, when I think
Of all the many millions
Who do not know
The sound of thy sweet name,
Who do not know
Who never can
Thy great salvation claim.

Then cries my heart,
O teach me, Lord, to care,
Until they know, how great thou art!
Then cries my heart,
O teach me, Lord, to care,
Until they know, how great thou art!

But when they know
That Jesus died to save them,
And when they know
The grace he can impart;
When Jesus shines
His love divine within them,
When he transforms
Their sinful, darkened heart:
Then they shall sing,
My Savior, God, to thee,
How great thou art,
How great thou art!

- ## Till Every Tribe Shall Hear

  (To the tune of *The Battle Hymn of the Republic*)
  How well we love the story
  Of the blessed Son of God,

How he purchased our redemption
When up Calv'ry's hill he trod,
How he told the ones who love him
They must tell his love abroad,
Till ev-ry tribe shall hear.

(Chorus)
Go to ev-ry tribe and nation
With the message of salvation,
Haste the joyful consummation
When ev-ry tribe shall hear.

But there are many millions
Who have never heard his name,
They've no hope of life eternal,
They cannot salvation claim;
For they do not know the message
Jesus told us to proclaim,
Till ev-ry tribe shall hear.

(Repeat chorus)

The Day of God is coming
When the Church of Christ shall stand
Face to face with Christ her Savior
In the blessed glory land;
And we each shall give our answer,
"Did you hasten my command—
That ev-ry tribe should hear?"

(Repeat chorus)

• He Is the King of Kings

(English)
He is the King of kings
He is the Lord of lords
His name is JESUS, JESUS, JESUS, JESUS
O, he is the King!

Following are pronunciations for the name *Jesus* in eight languages other than English. Try simply singing this chorus in English but substituting the other languages' pronunciation of *Jesus*.

(Spanish)
Cristo
Pronunciation: Cree-sto

(Russian)
Iesus
Pronunciation: Ee-ee-soos

(Japanese)
Iesu
Pronunciation: Yah-soo

(Swahili)
Yesu
Pronunciation: Yey-soo

(Hebrew)
Yeshua
Pronunciation: Y'shua

(Arabic)
Yaso'a
Pronunciation: Yah-so

(French)
Jésus
Pronunciation: Zhay-suee

(Hindi)
Pronunciation: Yee-soo

• I Have Decided to Follow Jesus

(English)
I have decided to follow Jesus (3x)
No turning back (2x).

(Hindi pronunciations—India)
Yee-soo kay pee-chay meh chull-nay luh-guh (3x)
Nuh low-doo-gah (2x).

(Eskimo pronunciations—Alaska)
Owl-lah-nik-tuu-nga maleeng-nyah-jee-gah Jesus (3x)
Oo-tee joo-tee joo-mee-nyeyt ngah (2x).

• Our God Is an Awesome God

Our God is an awesome God,
He reigns from heaven above,
With wisdom, power and love,
Our God is an awesome God!

(Missions verse)
Our God is a faithful God,
He keeps his promises,
To reach all nations,
Our God is a faithful God!

- **Jesus Loves the Little Children**

  Jesus loves the little children,
  All the children of the world.
  Red and yellow, black, and white,
  They are precious in His sight.
  Jesus loves the little children of the world.

  (Missions verse)
  Jesus loves the unreached children,
  All the unreached children of the world.
  Muslims, Buddhists, and Hindus,
  Chinese, tribals need him too.
  Jesus loves the unreached children of the world.

- **Hallelu, Hallelu**

  (English)
  Boys: Hallelu, Hallelu, Hallelu, Hallelujah!
  Girls: Praise ye the Lord!
              (Repeat both parts)
  Girls: Praise ye the Lord!
  Boys: Hallelujah!
              (Repeat both parts 2x)
  All: Praise ye the Lord!

  (Spanish)
  Boys: Hallelu, Hallelu, Hallelu, Hallelujah!
  Girls: Gloria a Dios!
              (Repeat)
  Girls: Gloria a Dios!
  Boys: Hallelujah!
              (Repeat 2x)
  All: Gloria a Dios!

(Spanish pronunciation)

Glow-ree-AH ah-Dee-OAS

(Russian pronunciations)

Boys:	Hallelu, Hallelu, Hallelu, Hallelujah!
Girls:	Ee-ee-sus, gaas-poat!
	(Repeat)
Girls:	Ee-ee-sus, gaas-poat!
Boys:	Hallelujah!
	(Repeat 2x)
All:	Ee-ee-sus, gaas-poat!

(Chinese pronunciations)

Boys:	Hallelu, Hallelu, Hallelu, Hallelujah!
Girls:	Zchan me choo!
	(Repeat)
Girls:	Zchan me choo!
Boys:	Hallelujah!
	(Repeat 2x)
All:	Zchan me choo!

(Swahili pronunciations)

Boys:	Hallelu, Hallelu, Hallelu, Hallelujah!
Girls:	Bwanna a see-fee-way!
	(Repeat)
Girls:	Bwanna a see-fee-way!
Boys:	Hallelujah!
	(Repeat 2x)
All:	Bwanna a see-fee-way!

(Luganda pronunciations—Uganda)

Boys:	Hallelu, Hallelu, Hallelu, Hallelujah!
Girls:	Ye-su ana-kupenda!
	(Repeat)

Girls:	Ye-su ana-kupenda!
Boys:	Hallelujah!
	(Repeat 2x)
All:	Ye-su ana-kupenda!

More Mission-Minded Choruses:

- He's Got the Whole World in His Hands

- This Little Light of Mine

- I Will Make You Fishers of Men

- If You're Happy and You Know It
  (Sing: "If you're blessed to be blessing . . .")

- In My Life, Lord, Be Glorified

- I Surrender All

- Hallelujah (sung all around the world)

- Lord, I Ask for the Nations (You Said)

- Shout to the Lord

🌐 TEACHING OPPORTUNITY

Taste International Foods

A mission-minded child is not a picky eater! When Jesus sent His followers on a mission outreach, he instructed them to "eat what is set before you" (Luke 10:8 NASB). If we want to train our children to be prepared for world missions, we need to train them to eat international foods. If your child is a picky eater, I encourage you to pray about changing your child-training philosophy in this area. Our children should be able to eat simple and rather bland foods

The Mission-Minded Child

like rice and fish (without complaining) and willing to at least try spicy and unusual foods.

No matter where you live, you can enjoy the fun of discovering delicious international cuisine. Search for foreign foods in your grocery store, try cooking an adventurous new dish, or experiment with an occasional (and perhaps daring) international snack.

Experience world culture at a local restaurant!

Take your family to visit an authentic international restaurant (Chinese, Middle Eastern, Indian, French, Italian, Mexican, Polynesian, etc.), and encourage your child to survey everything about the atmosphere—not only the taste of the food but also the music, decorations, and culture. As you observe, be especially on the lookout for indications of the owner's religion.

You and your child could even go to an international restaurant with a specific plan to share about Jesus. For example, if you are going to eat at a Chinese restaurant, you could bring along the *JESUS* film in a prominent Chinese language (such as Mandarin), a Chinese Bible, or a copy of "The Four Spiritual Laws" in Chinese (printed off the Internet). Most likely you will meet a waiter, hostess, or owner who speaks Chinese. Your gift (combined with a friendly testimony, your family's good manners, a nice tip, and your prayers) could lead to his or her salvation.

International Recipe Ideas:

- Mexico/Latin America:
  Tacos, Nachos, Tortillas, Spanish Rice

- Native America:
  Corn, Popcorn, Cornbread, Fish

- Western Europe:
  Spaghetti, Calzone, Greek Salad, German Sausage

- Eastern Europe:
  Borscht (beet and cabbage soup), Boiled Eggs, Dark Bread

- Middle East:
  Israeli Unleavened Bread, Lamb, Couscous, Pita Bread,
  Falafel (ground chickpeas shaped into balls and fried)

- Africa:
  Bananas, Pineapple, Peanuts, Rice, Boiled Potatoes, Matoke
  (mashed steamed bananas)

- Asia:
  Rice (try eating it with chopsticks!), Egg Rolls, Curried
  Chicken, Sushi, Stir-fry

Funny Missions Stories to Read Aloud to Children

Throughout the years, our family's international travels have led to amusing encounters, humorous misunderstandings, and hilarious adventures. When we have an opportunity to share about world missions, we often enjoy sharing a few of our "funny" missions stories. Although international missions work often means adjusting to curious cuisine and challenging conditions, it can also be extremely fun. Our family has enjoyed Polynesian snorkeling, European museums, African safaris, Middle Eastern camel "excursions," South American professional soccer games, and Australian boat rides. Take our word for it—or better yet, try it yourself—missions is definitely not boring!

— 👫 FROM MY CHILDREN'S PERSPECTIVE —

"GRASSHOPPERS FOR THANKSGIVING?"

By Joshua, at age thirteen

"So, what did *you* eat for Thanksgiving?"

A few days ago, during the week of Thanksgiving, my dad and I were across the world to Uganda, East Africa, holding evangelistic outreaches in remote cities out in the middle of nowhere. It was my second Thanksgiving holiday outside of America. But this time was really different.

In Africa, most people eat the same foods over and over again; at least we sure did. Day after day, meal after meal, we had overcooked rice, matoke (mashed steamed bananas), and a few chunks of tough meat and guts. But for Thanksgiving we had a "special" African treat. Along with our standard food, we were given a plate full of greasy fried *grasshoppers*!! They were about two inches long, with the legs and head still on.

As I stared at these insects, thoughts flashed through my brain. I imagined all the yummy food my brothers and sisters were eating at Grandma's house: turkey and pumpkin pie, mashed potatoes and gravy. I also remembered a time I had eaten big bugs before (at a kid's camp when I was bribed with a bunch of candy). It wasn't so hard to chug down an insect just once or twice on a dare, but this was different. It was Thanksgiving—and I was hungry!

Actually, they didn't taste that bad. As I took my first bite, they reminded me of a cross between popcorn and shrimp—crunchy on the outside and a little gooey on the inside. Soon I was eating one after the other, even throwing them in the air and catching them in my mouth. I must have eaten about sixty of them by the time I was done!

By the way, the ministry went well that night. We preached to thousands of people . . . and I felt just like John the Baptist!

THE SNICKERS BAR AND THE ANTS

By Carol Higgins, missionary to Africa

My husband, Bob, actually found a Snickers bar for me three days ago. I ate half of it and put the other half in the "pass-through" window between the kitchen and dining room—safe from dog and man, right?

The next day I was doing some mending for the children at the orphanage and got so sleepy I could hardly keep my eyes open. I thought about the treasured half Snickers bar and that it would wake me up. I got it, and not that I play with my food, but there is a certain technique I have for eating a Snickers. You know, eat the bottom first, then the caramel, and then the nuts—and, of course, savor every bite.

Well, I noticed a tickling on my fingers. Hmmmm . . . ants.

Then my face was being tickled by the same critters. I looked at my chewed-on candy bar and it was crawling with tiny little ants.

"Oh gross!" I thought as I was in the middle of a savory chew. Spit it out? My precious chocolate? How much ant-covered chocolate had I eaten? Give in to a couple hundred little ants? No way! I knocked the remaining bar on my sewing table; squashed the little buggers off the table, my face, and my hand; inspected it thoroughly; and enjoyed my remaining Snickers as systematically as I had begun: bottom to top.

My Bob thinks I have been in Africa too long. Maybe so!

 ## THE FILIPINO CURE FOR FLEAS

Our family was in a remote Filipino village on one of our first missionary trips, and the national pastor hosting us was very nervous.

"I've never hosted foreigners and don't know what to feed you," he said.

"Oh, we're easy to please," we responded naively. "Just relax; we'll eat whatever you put before us."

A few minutes later the pastor introduced us to the church women who were going to be cooking our food. One of them was eating this very different looking egg. It was black; and as she cracked it open, she started tugging at the insides—pulling out a black embryonic chick!

We found out that *balut* (a fertilized duck egg with a nearly-developed embryo that is boiled and eaten in the shell) was a common Filipino food . . . and we were nervous.

The people gave us an esteemed room in the village—the only room with a rug. Unfortunately, the rug was totally infested with fleas; and within a few days my legs were covered with flea bites.

When the pastor saw the bug bites, he said, "Oh, that is terrible. We must do something about those fleas biting you. Yes, there is only one thing to do."

"What's that?" we asked.

"Well, we must *eat the dog*. I was going to save it for a party, but I think we must eat it now."

A few days later, Jon came into our room. "Guess what we're having for dinner," he said with a raised eyebrow.

Not balut, I hoped. (I didn't know if I was *that* good of a missionary yet.)

I went to visit the church women and to see our menu for myself. These precious ladies were cutting up some strange white-looking meat. When I asked what it was, they talked among themselves in their Filipino language of Tagolog and then went to find someone who could interpret.

A few minutes later one woman came in and distinctly pronounced with wonderful enunciation the new English word she had just learned.

"Dog," she said.

"Dog?" I timidly asked, as my mind whirled with memories of special pets from my childhood.

The woman clarified herself: "Yes. You know—Ruff! Ruff!"

Yes, I knew far too well. But that's what we and our kids had for dinner that night. Our menu actually consisted of nearly-raw dog meat and fried dog intestines.

And we still had fleas!

 NEVER SHINE A FLASHLIGHT DOWN THE PIT!

"The Pit" is unlike anything you have likely experienced. It is totally different than a camp porta-potty and has absolutely no resemblance to a typical American bathroom. Not one home decorating magazine is displayed in a basket to read at your leisure, not one pretty towel hangs on a shiny silver bar, and fluffy coordinating bathmats are nowhere to be seen.

The Pit is a cement or mud cubicle with a weathered wooden door, a six-inch square hole in the ground, and an unforgettable "aroma"—all above a very, very deep pit.

One night we were in a remote African village dominated by demonic witchcraft. It was late . . . and dark; and a while after the evening ministry time was over our outreach team got rolling in one of those funny, middle-of-the-night conversations. The topic turned to some very practical missionary advice: "Be sure to *never* shine your flashlight down the Pit!" (Have you ever watched that scene from *Raiders of the Lost Ark* when Indiana Jones throws a torch down into the forbidden tomb and sees what he dreaded the most—the floor alive with snakes?! I think you get the picture. The Pit is often swarming above with flies; and in the unknown depths below, it's alive . . . with no one knows what!)

We all were laughing hysterically, including me . . . until I realized I had to "go," and it just couldn't wait until morning.

I got out my flashlight and went out into the darkness, through the rain—all by myself to the Pit. By this time, nothing seemed funny anymore.

I was very tired and wouldn't have minded those fluffy coordinating bathmats. As I neared the "aroma," I tried to decide my strategy. How could I go about using the Pit without shining the flashlight down?

When I arrived, I quickly threw open the rickety door—and barged in upon the biggest rat I had ever seen in my life! (With its tail it must have been nearly two feet long!) I wish I could say I was your strong, unflinching woman; but I screamed and just stood there, soaking wet, crying in the dark.

My precious husband, Jon, came to my rescue, got rid of the creature, made sure the coast was clear, then stood guard to make sure I was protected.

I bravely reentered the Pit with my flashlight, while my husband reentered his comical, slightly mischievous mood. He told our team to come watch something funny as he rolled a rock toward me under the Pit's door. My reaction did not let them down. I thought the rat was attacking me and I totally freaked out.

Everyone (except me!) thought it was the funniest joke of the evening!

 FIRE IN THE HOLE!

My brother participated in an African mission trip and went to use the same Pit where I had seen the giant rat. There were actually two cement stalls with a common hole down below. While he was on one side, one of our African friends wanted to bless our team by trying to clean up the Pit and getting rid of all the bugs. She tied banana leaves together, lit them on fire, and lowered them down the hole in the adjacent stall. But all the gases down below were so strong it caused an explosion, sending fire up both holes!

My brother instantly came bounding out of his stall, pulling up his pants and screaming, "Fire in the hole!"

THE BRIGHT-RED BLAZER

My husband used to have a recurring embarrassing dream. Jon would dream that as he got up to preach he would look down and realize he had nothing on but a red suit jacket!

After years of having this funny bad dream, he was preaching in a village of the Karamajong tribe in northern Uganda—an isolated people group who wear very little clothing. One afternoon a man came to Jon for ministry. He was clothed in nothing but a bright-red polyester blazer, with sleeves so short they came all the way up to his elbows! The man plopped down right in front of everyone with seemingly no realization of how naked (and funny) he looked.

It reminded my husband of his dream, which, fortunately, he never had again.

FUNNY QUESTIONS

Here are a couple of actual questions asked at a village marriage conference in East Africa. The missionaries found it quite hard to keep a straight face. How would you respond if someone asked you these questions?

Q. "Once a month I buy my wife a bar of sweet-smelling soap, but she still smells like a beast. What do I do?"

Q. "Every time my wife is pregnant, she acts like she is demon-possessed. What do I do?"

Another funny question occurred during a Christian teaching seminar in an isolated island village in the Philippines. My friends were the visiting missionaries when a national pastor asked if they could sing the song about the "magic tree."

"I'm sorry," our missionary friend responded, "but I'm afraid I've never heard that one before. Would you mind leading it for us?"

Immediately (and with much gusto) the young pastor began singing their church's very original rendition of Jack Hayford's popular worship chorus, "Majesty":

Magic tree, worship His magic tree,

Uncle Jesus, be all glory, honor and praise!

My missionary friends chuckled, realizing these remote Filipino believers must have thought the chorus referred to God's miraculous power through the cross of our Lord Jesus Christ.

REMOTE VILLAGERS VISIT THE BIG CITY

Over the years, we have had some interesting experiences bringing remote villagers out of the bush for the first time in their lives. It has been interesting to experience our own culture through new eyes. Those who have always lived near the equator often wonder if the world is coming to an end when daylight lasts so long in the summer. Others look totally lost and puzzled as they wander down the dog food aisle at the grocery store.

Reactions to our many food choices are sometimes comical. Most have never imagined so many different foods. Once, at a buffet restaurant, an African villager accidentally loaded his plate with plastic grapes from the display table, along with a helping of jelly beans covered with chicken gravy. Another time, a national pastor (who had never eaten green vegetables) saw my husband fixing a large salad and said, "Oh no, my brother, that is the food of a goat!"

— 👫 FROM MY CHILDREN'S PERSPECTIVE —

"COMPANY'S COMING!"
By Christi Dunagan, at age fourteen

MOM: Christi, we have company over often, including many missionary families, and you are a tremendous help. From your perspective as my teenage daughter, and from a practical point of view, what does "missionary hospitality" mean to you?

CHRISTI: Well, it means I'll have to do more dishes (without complaining), wash my sheets (making sure I've got matching pillowcases), clean my closet (usually two feet deep in clothes), get rid of all my little sister's messes and all my junk in the bathroom . . . and it's all got to be done really *fast* because usually our company's coming any minute!

It means that after a "sit-down, nicer-than-normal" dinner, I'll be in charge of keeping all the little kids quiet while the adults are visiting; and then, when it's time for bed, I'll "get" to sleep on the floor in my little brother's room (with a smile)!

When people from Africa or India come over, they usually think my bedroom is like a royal guesthouse! It reminds me of how much I have to be thankful for and how much I usually take for granted.

Sometimes our visitors have never seen a dishwasher, or a grocery store. One time we all were laughing so hard with our Ugandan friend when he couldn't figure out how a person could fit inside the little talking menu board at the Burger King drive-through! (Our national friend was laughing harder than any of us!) International guests have stood watching in amazement through an entire washing machine cycle—when the lid was up!

It can be interesting, and challenging, to hear exciting stories about how people have helped orphan children or about how missionaries have started Bible schools. It's fun also to have special speakers from church stay at our house (like groups from Teen Mania or Master's Commission). Many times these ministers have really encouraged me to want to do something more for God with my life.

When we welcome others into our home, especially other missionaries, it's not just a lot of work, and an exercise in patience—it's actually missionary training!

— 👫 FROM MY CHILDREN'S PERSPECTIVE —

"MY MOST-MEMORABLE COMMUNITY SERVICE PROJECT"
By Patrick Dunagan, age fifteen

As the last sheets of metal were nailed on, I took a step back to observe the finished product. It was a very simple building: many strong beams holding up a metal roof, and not even any walls. But as I saw the project near completion, I remember the tremendous satisfaction and happiness I felt.

But why be so satisfied over such a simple structure?

To understand how I felt, one must first know where I was. I wasn't in a poor neighborhood of my hometown or even in a big city slum but on the other side of the world, on a remote island in Lake Victoria. During this mission trip to Africa with my dad, I had seen many other island communities, but when we arrived at this particular island I was appalled at the living conditions. All the islands were poor and dirty, but this one left the others far behind. The village was made up of about one thousand people living in cramped, makeshift huts of grass, mud, and old garbage bags. Sewage ran down the narrow paths between the huts. Most children had little or no clothes. The horrible stench made me wonder how anyone could live there.

For them, that small, humble structure was a big event. Now their little island had its first real building, a church and community center for worship, practical health instruction, and teaching.

That night, as I boarded the dugout canoe, I knew God's impact on that little island would be felt for years.

(Note: On this mission outreach, Patrick traveled by a rugged canoe to help establish new churches on four remote Ugandan islands in Lake Victoria.)

— 👫 FROM MY CHILDREN'S PERSPECTIVE —

"EVANGELISM WITH THE *EVANGECUBE*****"
By Daniel Dunagan, age twelve

Dozens of Ugandan children were crowded around me as I climbed onto the back of our pickup truck. It was my very first mission trip, and now it was my turn to preach.

As I held up a big *EvangeCube*, I started to share about God's plan of salvation. I talked about Jesus; and phrase by phrase, an interpreter translated the message. Everyone stared intently. They were interested to see how the cube worked, and they were really interested in the message of God's salvation.

The *EvangeCube* is a really cool tool and it's easy to use. It's especially helpful when I'm sharing about how Jesus is the only way to heaven. As I got to the *EvangeCube* picture of "the cross as the bridge" to God, I asked the kids if any of them wanted to receive Jesus Christ as their Lord and Savior. Dozens of hands went up, and it was exciting to lead them in a prayer of salvation. With the *EvangeCube*, evangelism is easy!

*** *EvangeCube* is a tool used to walk people through the Gospel presentation using pictures. The blocks are flipped in different directions to show man's separation from God all the way to his sacrifice and resurrection from the tomb.

🌐 TEACHING OPPORTUNITY

Twenty (More) Ideas to Make Missions Fun

1. Put together a world map puzzle.

2. Learn to eat with chopsticks.

3. Check out a library book on origami art and experiment with this fun craft of Japanese paper-folding.

4. Buy (or make) a piñata and have a Mexican-theme party.

5. Have younger children dress up in international costumes, go outdoors, and play "Let's be a missionary!" (For older children, have a party with an international theme and give prizes for the best costumes.)

6. Learn to draw a few Chinese characters.

7. Collect international postage stamps.

8. Look up international time zones for major cities around the world and set several clocks at these times.

9. Make international flag posters. (Have your child decorate international flags and hang them from the ceiling.)

10. Look in the library or on the Internet for fun instructions on how to play a foreign game (like African *mancala*).

11. Send a quick and encouraging e-mail to a missionary. (Better yet, send a handwritten letter or a small care package!)

12. Listen to international music.

13. Watch an inspiring international movie (such as the classic film, *The Inn of the Sixth Happiness*).

14. Visit a local travel agency (or a travel agency on the Internet). Browse through international travel packages.

15. Type a personal letter to a foreign embassy asking for a tourist information packet about their country. (Check out foreign embassy websites on the Internet.)

16. Make a playdough relief map of a foreign country on a piece of cardboard. (Recipe: 1 cup flour, 1 cup salt, water to mix)

17. Look up information about a specific country on the Internet.

18. Sit on the couch and listen to an inspiring missionary biography (such as a story from *Hero Tales* or a Trailblazer book).

19. Visit the children's section of your local library and check out several books about a particular country.

20. Make "missionary passports."

🌐 TEACHING OPPORTUNITY

Make a Mission-Minded "Passport"

As your child learns about various areas of the world, a fun idea is to chart this progress on a special "passport."

Instructions:

1. What you need:

a photocopy of the passport pages displayed on the following pages, your child's photo, scissors, glue, colored construction paper, blank white paper, yarn, hole puncher, clear packing tape, and stapler (For fun, add international stickers or stamps.)

2. What to do:

Have your child cut out the passport pages along the dotted lines and glue these pieces to a passport-sized booklet (made from a half-piece of colored construction paper with blank white pages stapled inside). Add your child's photo to the appropriate box, and for strength and durability cover the entire passport with clear packing tape. Punch a hole in the top left corner, and insert a piece of yarn or cording so your child can wear the passport around his or her neck.

3. How to use this passport:

As your child learns about an area of the world, stamp the passport with a culturally appropriate rubber stamp, international flag or globe-oriented sticker, or a foreign postage stamp—all available at most teacher supply stores. This passport can be used to keep track of achievements such as Bible memory or Bible reading progress, or to record a child's personal prayer time as he or she "travels" around the world through intercession.

Cut and paste onto cover of passport (made from a folded piece of construction paper).

PASSPORT

Citizen of God's Kingdom

Cut and paste onto front inside page of passport (on white paper stapled inside).

Mission-Minded Child's Passport Number:

Last Name:

First Name:

Nation of Birth:

Birthday: _____ / _____ / _____   Born Again? (yes/no/unsure) _____

Boy or Girl? _____   Age: _____

Home Address: _____

Phone: _____   E-mail: _____

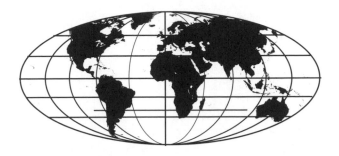

I'm a Mission-Minded Child

_____

SIGNATURE OF BEARER *(Sign your name here)*

 Cut each of these squares and paste onto any page inside of passport (on white paper stapled inside).

Our Great Commision:

"Go into all the world and preach the Gospel to every creature."

(Words of JESUS CHRIST from Mark 16:15)

THE WHOLE WORLD NEEDS JESUS

By Ann Dunagan

All over the world,
Far away and quite near,
There are millions of people who all need to hear
Of the message of Jesus,
But someone must GO,
And preach the Good News, so the whole world will know!

In God's eyes,
Each person is wonderfully made,
So to witness and share
We should not be afraid.
With the power of His Spirit,
We can be bold!
For the gospel to everyone
Must be told!

Others may have a different color of skin,
Or they may look real strong, or too tall, or too thin.
Their hair may be curly, or wavy, or straight,
But whatever the case, you had better not wait!

The whole world needs Jesus,
Each one needs to hear.
We must all share the news
Till it's reached every ear!

Some folks may be almost a hundred years old,
And they may live in places all icy and cold.
Or they may be real young,

'Bout the same age as you,
And live in the tropics
With seas warm and blue!
They might live in a mansion
Of silver and gold,
Or in a small shack
Made of tin that's real old.

Their words may sound strange,
Speaking French or Chinese,
Or Hebrew, or Russian, or perhaps Japanese!
But no matter what languages others may know,
They may not know Jesus,
So someone must GO!!
And although we're as different
As black is to white,
Each person is precious in Jesus' sight.

Their food may not be what you usually eat:
Some eat raw fish and rice
Or fried chicken feet.
Others eat monkeys,
Or snakes and cooked dogs,
And in some places people are known to eat FROGS!
But it's funny, you know,
'Cause some food that YOU eat
Tastes just awful to them,
Though to you it is sweet.

Your water may come from a faucet turned 'round,
But their water could come from a hole in the ground.
And their bed could be simply a mat on the floor,
While you have a mattress and pillows galore.

Yes, inside every home, some have less,
Some have more,
But people need Jesus behind every door.
Each person is different,
No two are the same;
But God knows everyone all by name.
He created us all from our head to our feet,
And made each person special—completely unique!
But there's one thing that's common and so very sad,
About every child, every mom, every dad.

All over the world,
From the young to the old,
Each person has sinned.
They've not done what God's told.

Some people lie,
Or they steal and they cheat;
Others make golden idols
And bow at their feet.
Some are selfish and greedy
—Not willing to share.
Others say there's no God (and pretend He's not there).

But no matter what terrible things folks have done,
God so loved the world
That He sent down His Son.
Jesus died on the cross for the sins of us all,
And forgives every one if on His name we call.

New life is a wonderful gift for each one.
But some still haven't *once*
Even heard what God's done!

Who will take the Good News
To all those far away?

Who will help?
Who will give?
Who will kneel down and pray?

We all have a part,
So just lend a hand,
Till the message of Jesus
Has reached every land.

The whole world needs Jesus,
Each one needs to hear.
We must all share the news
Till it's reached every ear!

Looking Back and Looking Ahead

Alone in the car. Hmmm . . . as a busy mother of seven, how often does *that* happen?

As I turned the corner and drove into the familiar campground, it felt significant—like I was supposed to be here to finish this book.

There are some moments in life that lend themselves to "thinking" about things: a child's high school graduation ceremony; a niece's wedding; a special memorial honoring a life well lived. It felt like one of those times.

After sharing hugs and hellos with dear Pastor Allan and Eunice Hanson (what faithful servants!), I lugged armloads of my computer paraphernalia into the red hilltop cabin and then headed out to look around. I reminisced and prayed in the little Victory Chapel, sat in the old Rotunda building, and quietly played "Lord, Have Your Way" on the piano.

Then I headed down that old dirt trail. I wondered if I could find the spot . . . and if I'd be able to recognize it.

And finally, there it was. As if time had stood still, I almost felt like I was a little girl again—as if God and I were meeting together to recall that special moment from my past.

Once again, I sat down on a log and listened to that stream rippling and gurgling beside me. The sun glistened as I looked toward the sky. *Wow,* I wondered, as I gazed up at those majestic pine and birch trees, *how much had those trees grown in thirty years?*

It was definitely "one of those moments."

It was thirty years ago . . . right about this time of the summer . . . right in this very spot . . . that the Lord "called" me to world missions.

I felt so overwhelmingly thankful. So inadequate. So grateful.

The sunbeams looked beautiful and the leaves looked remarkably green. For a long and lingering moment, I simply basked in the Lord's presence.

As a child, this was the place where I had first "heard" His voice and His calling for me to go to the nations, which had now become a reality. Like a whirlwind of memories, jumbled thoughts flooded my mind: the moment I met my husband; the births of our children; smuggling Bibles into China; airplane trips and Filipino jeepney rides; fun birthday parties and big church potlucks; preaching to multitudes; and dancing in an African downpour!

I felt more in love than ever—in love with my handsome husband, in love with our awesome kids, and totally in love with Jesus. I am truly a blessed woman, a happy mommy, and probably the proudest wife in the world (in a good way!). I love sharing how my daring sweetheart had the opportunity to preach the gospel on every continent, including Antarctica, all within this last year! God has been *so* good!

Looking Ahead . . .

A few weeks from now, I'm actually heading overseas to a remote village in Africa for a women's conference. After years of staying home, I'm looking forward to going again. God's plans and purposes have surpassed my childhood dreams. And I know He has more!

For each child we influence and for their generation (and for you!), God has a perfect plan and a destiny. He has purposes as unique as each personality and adventures that may be enjoyable . . . or perhaps very difficult.

He yearns for our children to be rock-solid in faith, bold in witness, and daring enough to live totally for His kingdom! He wants to spare our children the heartaches of disobedience, the regrets of midlife, and the despair of wasted years. Most of all, God sees a lost generation—masses of young people scattered throughout the earth—desperately needing His love!

There's a whole world out there: dirty boys kicking an old ball around a dusty South American field, a little girl lonely for a friend, a middle-school kid drowning in his boredom, an old man dying, and multitudes of precious babies being born.

Who will go to them? And who will raise the spiritual leaders of tomorrow?

> Then the word of the LORD came to me, saying: "Before I formed you in the womb I knew you; before you were born I sanctified you; I ordained you a prophet to the nations."
>
> Then said I: "Ah, Lord God! Behold, I cannot speak, for I am a youth."
>
> But the LORD said to me: "Do not say, 'I am a youth,' for you shall go to all to whom I send you, and whatever I command you, you shall speak. Do not be afraid of their faces, for I am with you to deliver you," says the LORD (Jeremiah 1:4–8).

These words were not just for me. The Lord is calling *your child*!

Recommended Resources

Missions and Prayer

- *From Akebu to Zapotec,* by June Hathersmith and Alice Roder (Wycliffe Bible Translators, 2002). This new alphabet book introduces children to twenty-six of the world's Bible-less people groups. Today most of the twenty-six people groups from Wycliffe's first alphabet book, *From Arapesh to Zuni,* published in 1986, have some part of the Bible in their language—demonstrating that prayer is powerful! Wycliffe Bible Translators: 1-800-992-5433, or www.wycliffe.org/catalog.

- *God's Got Stuff to Do! And He Wants Your Help* (Pioneers, 2003). This thirteen-week curriculum was created to expose kids to what can be done to help share Jesus with the nations. It includes a teacher's resource kit and a student booklet (a journal-style Bible study that leads kids to discover opportunities to go, send others, pray, give, welcome internationals in this country, and connect with others for service). Also available from Pioneers is the *Kids Around the World Teacher's Resource Kit* and *Kids Around the World THUMB Teacher's Resource Kit.*

- *Kids' Prayer Cards* (Pioneers, 2006). More than just cards, this pack is a window into the lives of kids around the world! Discover what they think is fun, exciting, and cool with these twenty-five colorful cards. People Group Cards give you a look at the lives of kids in different cultures and Activity Cards give you everything you need to paint tribal art, eat their food, and even meet and make friends with those in your own neighborhood. This prayer card set is built on the T.H.U.M.B. acrostic and the cards are shaped like the letters: T is for Tribal, H is for Hindu, U is for Unreligious (or atheist), M is for Muslim, and B is for Buddhist.

- *Operation World: 21ˢᵗ Century Edition,* by Patrick Johnstone and Jason Mandryk (Authentic Publishing, 2001). With over 2 million copies in print, this handbook for global prayer is highly recommended as a resource for mission-minded families. Packed with information about every country in the world, this book is inspiring fuel for prayer.

- *Window on the World,* by Daphne Spraggett and Jill Johnstone (Angus Hudson, Ltd., 2002 by Authentic Media). This children's accompaniment to *Operation World* is an outstanding tool for parents and teachers and my number one recommendation for your child. Filled with stunning full-color glossy photographs, this A to Z guide to one hundred countries and people groups will provide an exciting learning experience and tool for prayer.

- *YWAM Personal Prayer Diary and Daily Planner* (YWAM Publishing, 2005). Every year YWAM produces a new daily planner, which includes illustrations of unreached people, highlights for prayer, maps, monthly calendars, and Scriptures. This is an excellent organizational tool for older children, teens, and adults.

- *Walking with God: The Young Person's Prayer Diary,* by Michelle Drake (YWAM Publishing, 2005). This energetic diary will encourage your child to establish the mission-minded discipline of daily prayer. With cartoon illustrations, practical Bible reading charts, world maps, prayer teaching highlights, and plenty of encouraging spaces for a young person to write, this tool is very child-friendly and highly recommended.

Missionary Biographies

- Christian Hall of Fame—www.Christianhof.org: an online resource highlighting many heroes of the Christian faith throughout history.

- *Christian Heroes: Then & Now,* by Janet and Geoff Benge (YWAM Publishing). This best-selling missionary biography series chronicles the exciting, challenging, and deeply touching true stories of ordinary men and women whose trust in God accomplished extraordinary exploits for His kingdom. An accompanying unit study curriculum guide is available.

- *From Jerusalem to Irian Jaya: A Biographical History of Christian Missions,* by Ruth Tucker (Zondervan, 2004). This excellent academic book (written for adults) has been revised and is now available in hardback. It examines the history of Christian missions by emphasizing personal biographies. With details, maps, photos, and charts, it is a helpful resource for home, church, or school.

- *Hero Tales,* by Dave and Neta Jackson (Bethany House). This treasury of true stories from the lives of Christian heroes contains valuable lessons that can be read alone or together for family or classroom devotions. Each of the four volumes consists of forty-five exciting and educational readings drawn from the lives of fifteen key Christian heroes. Geared for ages six to twelve, these books include questions and missionary portraits.

- *Heroes for Young Readers* (YWAM Publishing). Many of the books in this series are mentioned in chapter 6. These illustrated books about famous missionaries are great for younger readers.

- *Heroes of the Faith* (Barbour Publishing). Written by Sam Wellman and other authors, this series covers men and women not traditionally written about in missionary series, like C. S. Lewis, Mother Teresa, and Billy Graham.

- *International Adventures,* by various authors (YWAM Publishing). These exciting classic and new missionary biographies have been collected and repackaged to reach a new generation. Every title emerges as a dramatic episode directed by the hand of God. Current titles include *Torches of Joy, A Cry from the Streets, Adventures in Naked Faith, Living on the Devil's Doorstep, Against All Odds, Tomorrow You Die, Dayuma: Life Under the Waorani Spears, Imprisoned in Iran, The Man with the Bird on His Head, Peace Child,* and *Lords of the Earth.*

- *Is That Really You, God?* by Loren Cunningham (YWAM Publishing, 2001; also available in hardback, by Chosen Books). This practical guide to hearing God's voice shows how an ordinary man who was committed to hearing and obeying God became the founder of the largest interdenominational mission organization in the world. Cunningham's extensive missionary travels have taken him to every country in the world, and his life of faith is an excellent contemporary example for our children. This book is a must-read!

- *Men and Women of Faith Series,* various authors (Bethany House). Written for older readers (seventh grade to adult).

- *Revolution in World Missions,* by K. P. Yohannan (Charisma House, 1995). A challenging book focused on raising and supporting national missionaries.

- The *By Faith Biography Series,* various authors (Ambassador-Emerald International). Designed with younger readers in mind.

- *The Life and Diary of David Brainerd,* by Philip E. Howard, edited by Jonathan Edwards (Baker, 1989).

- *Through Gates of Splendor,* by Elisabeth Elliot (Tyndale, revised edition, 1986), and *The Journals of Jim Elliot,* edited by Elisabeth Elliot (Revell, 2002). Inspiring biographies of Jim Elliot.

- *Trailblazer Series,* by Dave and Neta Jackson (Bethany House). These exciting stories of adventure and faith will entertain your children while teaching them about Christian heroes of the past. This series has won enthusiastic support from families and teachers. Geared for ages eight to thirteen, these missionary biographies are perfect for children to read themselves.

- *Richard Wurmbrand: Voice in the Dark,* by Carine MacKenzie (Christian Focus Publications, 1997).

- Wholesome Words—www.wholesomewords.org: The "Children's Corner" includes many delightful missionary stories for oral reading.

Missions Adventures, Fiction

- *Reel Kids Adventures Series,* by David Gustaveson (YWAM Publishing). Each book in this high-paced international adventure series has a missions theme. The series is written for older children or young adults. Titles include *The Missing Video* (Cuba), *Mystery at Smokey Mountain* (Philippines), *The Mysterious Case* (Colombia), and seven other exciting volumes!

World Missions: Inspiration and Teaching

- *The Passion for Souls,* by Oswald J. Smith (The Chaucer Press, Lakeland Edition, 1983). A powerful missions classic.

- *The Challenge of Missions,* by Oswald J. Smith (Eternal Word Ministries, reprint edition, 2003). An outstanding missions classic.

- *The Missions Addiction: Capturing God's Passion for the World,* by David Shibley (Charisma House, 2001). Inspiring and challenging summary of the need for world missions today.

- *Teaching with God's Heart for the World—Volume I & II,* by Ann Dunagan (Family Mission Vision Enterprises, 1995). Limited availability. A day-by-day unit study guide to incorporate God's heart for world missions into nearly every subject. Designed to give an overview of world history and an overview of world geography all within one school year. Includes many practical ideas, crafts, recipes, and more (www.harvestreport.net).

Other Missions Resources

Dare to Be a Daniel (D2BD): www.daretobeadaniel.com

Extreme Devotion, by The Voice of the Martyrs (Thomas Nelson, 2001).

Global Expeditions: www.globalexpeditions.com

Jesus Freaks, Volume 1: Stories of Those Who Took a Stand for Jesus, by dc Talk and The Voice of the Martyrs (Bethany House, 1999). This book tells the incredible stories of brave Christians from both long ago and in recent history who were willing to surrender everything (even their lives) to follow Jesus. Because of its graphic and vivid examples, it is not recommended for young children; however, with adult supervision it is extremely powerful for older children and especially appropriate for teens and young adults. See also the sequel: *Jesus Freaks, Volume 2: Stories of Revolutionaries Who Changed Their World* (Bethany House, 2002).

Operation Christmas Child: www.samaritanspurse.org

Teen Mania: www.teenmania.com

Teen Missions: www.teenmissions.org

"The Four Spiritual Laws": www.greatcom.org/laws/languages.html

The JESUS Film Project: www.jesusfilm.org

The Voice of the Martyrs: www.persecution.com

YWAM (Youth With A Mission) King's Kids: www.ywam.org and www.kkint.net

Wycliffe Bible Translators: www.wycliffe.org

Notes

Opening quotes

Quotes by Hudson Taylor, at age five, and his parents, Mr. and Mrs. James Hudson Taylor: from *Hudson Taylor in Early Years: The Growth of a Soul*, by Dr. and Mrs. Howard Taylor, published by the China Inland Mission, printed in Ann Arbor, MI: Edwards Brothers, Inc., 1943, p. 37.

Chapter 1

Story of Hannah and Samuel from 1 Samuel 1–3.

Chapter 2

"A Passion for Souls"—Herbert G. Tovey, 1888. Words of this hymn are in public domain.

Chapter 3

Missions statistics compiled from the *World Christian Encyclopedia,* edited by David B. Barrett, George T. Kurian, and Todd M. Johnson (Oxford University Press, 2001); *700 Hundred Plans to Evangelize the World,* by David Barrett (New Hope, 1988); *Revolution in World Missions,* by K. P. Yohannan (Gospel for Asia); and a brochure, *The Glaring Injustice of 21st Century Missions* (www.missionindia.org).

"A Hundred Thousand Souls"—Author unknown; poem and quote excerpted from *The Harvest Call,* by T. L. Osborn (Tulsa: The Voice of Faith, Inc., 1953), p. 109. Used by permission of Osborn International.

"The Little Starfish"—Original source unknown; retold by Ann Dunagan.

Chapter 4

Bible chart—Bible verses organized and compiled by Ann Dunagan and Andrew Sloan.

Chapter 6

Missionary biographical information compiled and adapted by Ann Dunagan from various sources, including:

Ann Dunagan, *Teaching with God's Heart for the World, Volume I & II.*

Elmer L. Towns, *The Christian Hall of Fame* (Grand Rapids: Baker, 1971).

Oliver Ransford, *David Livingstone: The Dark Interior* (New York: St. Martin's, 1978), p. 14.

Ruth A. Tucker, *From Jerusalem to Irian Jaya: A Biographical History of Christian Missions* (Grand Rapids: Zondervan, 2004).

Sherwood Eddy, *Pathfinders of the World Missionary Crusade* (New York: Abingdon-Cokesbury, 1945), p. 125.

Will Durant, *The Reformation,* Volume 6 of *The Story of Civilization* (New York: Simon & Schuster, 1957), p. 204.

Current missionary biographies were all checked with each minister's official ministry website, updated 2004–2007.

Missionary statistics checked with online information from the William Carey Library, 2005.

Classic Missionary Excerpts:

"A 'Big Man' Meets a 'Real Man'"—Loren Cunningham, *Winning God's Way* (Seattle: YWAM Publishing, 1988), pp. 46–49. Used by permission of Loren Cunningham and Youth With A Mission.

"The Christian Magna Carta"—Loren Cunningham, excerpted from *Target Earth: The Necessity of Diversity in a Holistic Perspective on World Mission,* by Frank Kaleb Jansen (Kailua-Kona, HA: University of the Nations, and Pasadena, CA: Global Mapping, 1989), p. 86. Used by permission of Loren Cunningham and Youth With A Mission.

"Did Not Your Forefathers Know?"—Mrs. J. H. Worcester Jr., *David Livingstone: First to Cross Africa with the Gospel* (Chicago: Moody Press, 1993), pp. 26–27.

"Dr. Duff's Appeal"—Oswald J. Smith, *The Challenge of Missions* (Waynesboro, GA: Operation Mobilization Literature Ministry, 1959), pp. 37–38. (This book is out of print but was reprinted in 2003 by Eternal Word Ministries.) Used by permission of The People's Church of Toronto, Canada, and the family of Oswald J. Smith.

"The Man in the Clouds"—Paul Eshleman, article excerpted from a JESUS Film Project monthly newsletter, 2003; used by permission of Paul Eshleman and the JESUS Film Project.

"Man of Mission—Man of Prayer"—Dr. and Mrs. Howard Taylor, *Hudson Taylor's Spiritual Secret* (Chicago: Moody Press, 1983), condensed from pp. 234–236.

"Only the Grace of God—Spear-Wielding Killer Now Church Elder"—David Shibley, *The Missions Addiction: Capturing God's Passion for the World* (Lake Mary, FL: Charisma House, 2001), pp. 199–200.

"Our Obligation"—Elmer L. Towns, *The Christian Hall of Fame* (Grand Rapids: Baker, 1971), p. 90. Original quote from William Carey's famous missions book entitled *An Enquiry into the Obligations of Christians to Use Means for the Conversion of the Heathens.*

"The Small Woman"—Alan Burgess, *The Small Woman: The Heroic Story of Gladys Aylward* (New York: E. P. Dutton & Co., Inc., 1957); excerpt from chapter 1.

Chapter 7

Various ideas in this chapter adapted from Jon and Ann Dunagan, *New Life in Jesus* (Hood River, OR: Harvest Ministry, 2000).

Chapter 8

Prayer ideas taken from personal missionary experiences and from the following sources:

Danny Lehman, *Before You Hit the Wall* (Seattle: YWAM Publishing, 1991).

James P. Shaw, senior editor, *Personal Prayer Diary and Daily Planner* (Seattle: YWAM Publishing, 1995), pp. 12–15, 192.

Chapter 9

"My Choice"—Bill McChesney, excerpted from *Winning God's Way,* by Loren Cunningham (Seattle: YWAM Publishing, 1988), pp. 47–49. Used by permission of Loren Cunningham and Youth With A Mission.

"Why We Should Give Money for Missions"—Missions statistics from *The World Christian Encyclopedia,* edited by David B. Barrett, George T. Kurian, and Todd M. Johnson (Oxford University Press, 2001); and *Revolution in World Missions,* by K. P. Yohannan (Altamonte Springs, FL: Charisma House, 1995), p. 129.

Chapter 11

Music and international ideas compiled and adapted from various sources, including:

Bev Gunderson, *Window to India, Window to Japan*, and *Window to Mexico* (Milaca, MN: Monarch Publishing, 1988).

Mary Branson, *Fun Around the World* (Birmingham: New Hope, 1992).

Phyllis Vos Wezeman and Jude Dennis Fournier, *Joy to the World* (Notre Dame, IN: Ave Maria Press, 1992).

Ruth Finley, *The Secret Search* (Mt. Hermon, CA: Crossroads Communications, 1990).

Kerry Lovering, *Missions Idea Notebook: Promoting Missions in the Local Church* (Scarborough, Ontario: SIM International Publications, 1984).

Special thanks to missionary friends Bob and Carol Higgins (of Path Ministries International, www.pathministries.net) for "The Snickers Bar and the Ants," and to John and Katy Ricards (missionaries to the island of Mindanao in the Philippines with Ministries to Christian Nationals) for the "Magic Tree" story.

Illustration Index

Chapter 1

Child's letter   Dunagan family

Child's illustration   Dunagan family

Chapter 4

Bible Chart 1   Ann Dunagan

Bible Chart 2   Ann Dunagan

Bible Chart 3   Ann Dunagan

Chapter 6

Ignatius   The Christian Hall of Fame. Canton Baptist Temple, Canton, OH. Used with permission. All rights reserved (nontransferable).

Polycarp   The Christian Hall of Fame. Canton Baptist Temple, Canton, OH. Used with permission. All rights reserved (nontransferable).

John Wycliffe   The Christian Hall of Fame. Canton Baptist Temple, Canton, OH. Used with permission. All rights reserved (nontransferable).

Martin Luther   Public domain

Count Zinzendorf   Public domain

David Brainerd   Public domain

George Liele   Jesse L. Boyd, *A Popular History of Baptists in America Prior to 1845* (New York: 1947).

William Carey   The Christian Hall of Fame. Canton Baptist Temple, Canton, OH. Used with permission. All rights reserved (nontransferable).

David Livingstone	Public domain
Hudson Taylor	The Christian Hall of Fame. Canton Baptist Temple, Canton, OH. Used with permission. All rights reserved (nontransferable).
Amy Carmichael	The Dohnavur Fellowship
John and Betty Stam	Overseas Missionary Fellowship. Used with permission. All rights reserved.
Gladys Aylward	Alan Burgess, *The Small Woman: The Heroic Story of Gladys Aylward* (New York: E. P. Dutton & Co., Inc., 1957).
Cameron Townsend	Wycliffe Bible Translators. Used with permission. All rights reserved.
Oswald J. Smith	People's Church, Toronto, Ontario. Used with permission of the family.
Alexander Duff	Public domain
Bill Bright	Campus Crusade for Christ. Used with permission. All rights reserved.
JESUS Film	Campus Crusade for Christ. JESUS Film. www.jesusfilm.org. All rights reserved.
Yonggi Cho	Full Gospel Central Church: Seoul, South Korea
Loren Cunningham	Youth With A Mission. Used with permission of YWAM and Loren Cunningham. All rights reserved.
Paul Rader	Public domain
Billy Graham	Billy Graham Evangelistic Association. Used with permission. All rights reserved (nontransferable).
Ron Luce	Teen Mania Ministries. Used with permission. All rights reserved.
Luis Palau	Luis Palau Evangelistic Association. Used with permission. All rights reserved.
Richard Wurmbrand	The Voice of the Martyrs. Used with permission. All rights reserved.
K. P. Yohannan	Gospel for Asia. Used with permission. All rights reserved.
Kanaabo	Harvest Ministry. Used with permission. All rights reserved.

Chapter 9

Chapter 10

Appendix

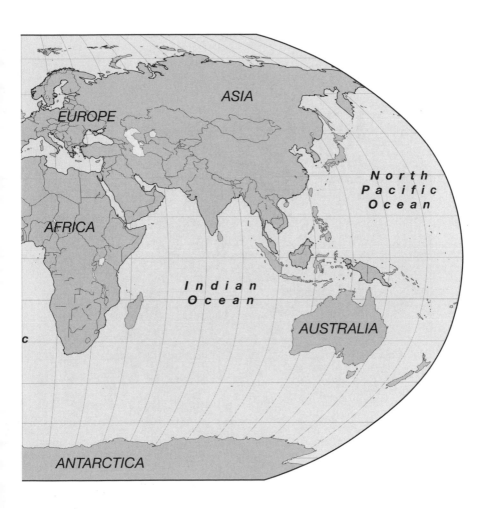

ASIA

EUROPE

North
Pacific
Ocean

AFRICA

Indian
Ocean

AUSTRALIA

c

ANTARCTICA

THE WORLD
ROBINSON PROJECTION
©2005 Geography Matters

www.geomatters.com

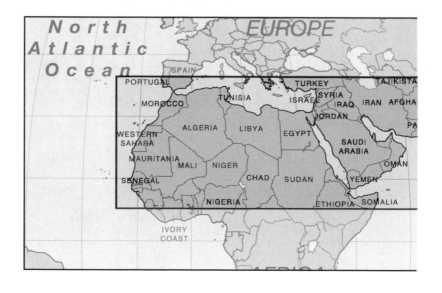

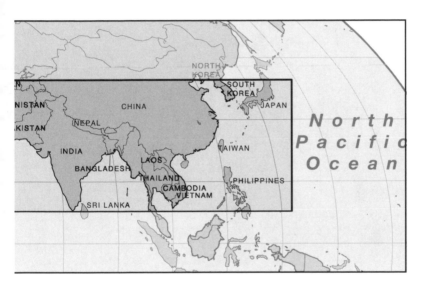

THE "10/40 WINDOW"
ROBINSON PROJECTION

www.geomatters.com